Accountability and Culture of School Teachers and Principals

Accountability and Culture of School Teachers and Principals studies the degree to which teachers and principals in eight countries view themselves as taking responsibility, working by clear standards, reporting transparently, and accepting feedback at work.

The book focuses on cultural values that explain variation in accountability levels of school educators, drawing on data from Canada, China, Hungary, Israel, the Netherlands, Spain, South Africa, and Zimbabwe. It addresses the question of whether cultural values, specifically collectivism and individualism, are related to teachers' and principals' external and internal accountability dispositions. It also explores the intriguing role of organizational support and key school personnel in school reforms across the world, providing a new way to understand school accountability.

The book will be of great interest for academics, post-graduate students, and scholars in the fields of education policy and international and comparative studies in education.

Zehava Rosenblatt is Professor Emerita in the Department of Leadership and Educational Policy at the University of Haifa, Israel. Her research is focused on ethical issues in teachers' work, such as personal accountability and absenteeism, as well as other related topics in teachers' organizational behavior.

Theo Wubbels is Professor Emeritus of Educational Sciences at Utrecht University, the Netherlands. His research interests developed in his career from the pedagogy of physics education, via problems of beginning teachers and teaching and learning in higher education to studies of learning environments and, especially, interpersonal relationships in education.

Routledge Research in Teacher Education

The Routledge Research in Teacher Education series presents the latest research on Teacher Education and also provides a forum to discuss the latest practices and challenges in the field.

Becoming Somebody in Teacher Education
Person, Profession and Organization in a Global Southern Context
Kari Kragh Blume Dahl

Professional Learning and Identities in Teaching
International Narratives of Successful Teachers
Edited by A. Cendel Karaman and Silvia Edling

Teacher Quality and Education Policy in India
Understanding the Relationship Between Teacher Education, Teacher Effectiveness, and Student Outcomes
Preeti Kumar and Alexander W. Wiseman

Teacher Educators and their Professional Development
Learning from the Past, Looking to the Future
Edited by Ruben Vanderlinde, Kari Smith, Mieke Lunenberg and Jean Murray

Accountability and Culture of School Teachers and Principals
An Eight-country Comparative Study
Zehava Rosenblatt and Theo Wubbels

For more information about this series, please visit: www.routledge.com/Routledge-Research-in-Teacher-Education/book-series/RRTE

Accountability and Culture of School Teachers and Principals
An Eight-country Comparative Study

Zehava Rosenblatt and Theo Wubbels

LONDON AND NEW YORK

First published 2021
by Routledge
2 Park Square, Milton Park, Abingdon, Oxon OX14 4RN

and by Routledge
52 Vanderbilt Avenue, New York, NY 10017

Routledge is an imprint of the Taylor & Francis Group, an informa business

© 2021 Zehava Rosenblatt and Theo Wubbels

The right of Zehava Rosenblatt and Theo Wubbels to be identified as authors of this work has been asserted by them in accordance with sections 77 and 78 of the Copyright, Designs and Patents Act 1988.

All rights reserved. No part of this book may be reprinted or reproduced or utilised in any form or by any electronic, mechanical, or other means, now known or hereafter invented, including photocopying and recording, or in any information storage or retrieval system, without permission in writing from the publishers.

Trademark notice: Product or corporate names may be trademarks or registered trademarks, and are used only for identification and explanation without intent to infringe.

British Library Cataloguing-in-Publication Data
A catalogue record for this book is available from the British Library

Library of Congress Cataloging-in-Publication Data
A catalog record for this book has been requested

ISBN: 978-1-138-49540-1 (hbk)
ISBN: 978-0-367-76205-6 (pbk)
ISBN: 978-1-351-02410-5 (ebk)

Typeset in Times New Roman
by Apex CoVantage, LLC

The book is dedicated to the memory of our late colleague and dear friend, Professor Lya Kremer-Hayon.

Theo Wubbels and Zehava Rosenblatt

This book is also dedicated to the memory of my late husband, Professor Meir Rosenblatt.

Zehava Rosenblatt

Contents

List of tables, figures, and appendices x
Contributing chapter authors xiv
Contributing researchers xv
Acknowledgments xix

1 Introduction 1
*Preoccupation with educational accountability
as a panacea for educational ills* 2
Development of accountability theory 4

**2 Teachers' and principals' accountability: theoretical
background** 6
Conceptualizing accountability 6
Accountability and cultural values 16
Accountability and organizational support 22

3 Study methods 26
JORIS G.J. BEEK, ZEHAVA ROSENBLATT, CHRIS PHIELIX,
AND THEO WUBBELS

Introduction 26
Data collection 27
Study measures 28
Analytical approach 31
Appendix 3.1: handling of missing data 35
*Appendix 3.2: the questionnaires used in the study
(English version)* 36

Appendix 3.3: psychometric and questionnaire position of study variables 49
Appendix 3.4: check on leveled structure teacher data 51
Appendix 3.5a: models for teachers' external accountability 53
Appendix 3.5b: models for teachers' internal accountability 58
Appendix 3.6a: models for teachers' accountability toward parents 63
Appendix 3.6b: models for teachers' accountability toward school management 68

4 Study findings 74
JORIS G.J. BEEK, ZEHAVA ROSENBLATT, AND THEO WUBBELS

Introduction 74
Accountability distribution 75
Cultural values distribution 88
Organizational support distribution 97
Prediction of teachers' and principals' external and internal accountability 101
Prediction of accountability: summary 121

5 Discussion of study findings 124
Introduction 124
The two dimensions of accountability: external and internal 124
Accountability audiences: parents and school management 128
Effect of principals' accountability on teachers' accountability 131
Predicting accountability by personal individualism and collectivism 131
Accountability at a country level 135
Organizational support as a predictor of accountability disposition 143

6 Concluding thoughts 147
Educators' accountability versus school accountability 147
Focus on internal accountability 148
Cultural values and accountability – theoretical and practical implications 149
The contingent role of the accountability audience 150
Team accountability: a future research direction 152

References 154
Index 164

Tables, figures, and appendices

Tables

3.1	Provinces or Regions in the Participating Countries and Number of Teachers and Principals	27
4.1	*Teachers'* Accountability	75
4.2	*Principals'* Accountability	76
4.3	Country Similarities and Differences on Teachers' External Accountability	78
4.4	Country Similarities and Differences on Teachers' Internal Accountability	79
4.5	Country Similarities and Differences on Principals' External Accountability	79
4.6	Country Similarities and Differences on Principals' Internal Accountability	80
4.7	*Teacher* Gender Differences for External Accountability, Means, Standard Deviations, T-Tests, and Effect Sizes	80
4.8	*Teacher* Gender Differences for Internal Accountability, Means, Standard Deviations, T-Tests, and Effect Sizes	81
4.9	*Principal* Gender Differences for External Accountability, Means, Standard Deviations, T-Tests, and Effect Size	82
4.10	*Principal* Gender Differences for Internal Accountability, Means, Standard Deviations, T-Tests, and Effect Size	82
4.11	Correlations Between Teacher and Principal Seniority and Accountability	83
4.12	Correlations of Accountability Toward Parents and School Management and General External Accountability	84
4.13	*Teachers'* Means and Standard Deviations of Accountability Toward Parents and School Management, T-Tests, and Effect Sizes	85

Tables, figures, and appendices xi

4.14 *Principals'* Means and Standard Deviations of Accountability Toward Parents and School Management, T-Tests, and Effect Sizes — 86
4.15 Teachers' and Principals' Means and Standard Deviations of Accountability Toward Parents, T-Tests, and Effect Sizes — 87
4.16 Teachers' and Principals' Means and Standard Deviations of Accountability Toward School Management, T-Tests, and Effect Sizes — 89
4.17 *Teachers'* Means and Standard Deviations of Cultural Values, T-Tests, and Effect Sizes for the Comparison of Individualism and Collectivism — 90
4.18 *Principals'* Means and Standard Deviations of Cultural Values, T-Tests, and Effect Sizes for Comparison of Individualism and Collectivism — 91
4.19 Country Similarities and Differences on Teachers' Individualism — 93
4.20 Country Similarities and Differences on Teachers' Collectivism — 93
4.21 Country Similarities and Differences on Principals' Individualism — 94
4.22 Country Similarities and Differences on Principals' Collectivism — 94
4.23 *Teacher* Gender Differences for Individualism, Means, Standard Deviations, T-Tests, and Effect Sizes — 95
4.24 *Teacher* Gender Differences for Collectivism, Means, Standard Deviations, T-Tests, and Effect Sizes — 95
4.25 *Principal* Gender Differences for Individualism Means, Standard Deviations, T-Tests, and Effect Sizes — 96
4.26 *Principal* Gender Differences for Collectivism Means, Standard Deviations, T-Tests, and Effect Sizes — 96
4.27 Correlations Between Teacher and Principal Seniority and Cultural Values — 97
4.28 *Teachers'* Means and Standard Deviations of Organizational Support by Gender, T-Tests, and Effect Sizes — 98
4.29 *Principals'* Means and Standard Deviations of Organizational Support by Gender, T-Tests, and Effect Sizes — 98
4.30 Country Similarities and Differences on *Teachers'* Organizational Support — 100
4.31 Country Similarities and Differences on *Principals'* Organizational Support — 100

xii Tables, figures, and appendices

4.32 Correlations Between Teachers' and Principals' Seniority and Organizational Support 100
4.33 Correlations Between Teacher Study Variables 102
4.34 Models for Predicting Teachers' External and Internal Accountability 104
4.35 Predictive Model for Teachers' External and Internal Accountability With Principals' External Respectively Internal Accountability as Predictor 107
4.36 Correlations Between Teacher Variables and Accountability Toward Parents and School Management 109
4.37 Prediction of Teachers' External Accountability Toward Parents and School Management 110
4.38 Predictive Model for Teachers' External Accountability Toward Parents and School Management With Principals' Parents or School Management Accountability Scores as Predictors 111
4.39 Correlations Between Principal Study Variables 115
4.40 Regression Models for Predicting Principals' Accountability Without and With Dummy Variables for Countries 116
4.41 Correlations Between Principal Variables and Accountability Toward Parents and School Management 118
4.42 Regression Models for Predicting Principals' Accountability Toward Parents and School Management Without and With Dummy Variables for Countries 119
5.1 Correlations of Teachers' and Principals' External and Internal Accountability Dispositions and Countries' In-Group Collectivism From the GLOBE Project 141

Figures

4.1 Teachers' External and Internal Accountability by Country 76
4.2 Principals' External and Internal Accountability by Country 77
4.3 Teachers' External Accountability Toward Parents and School Management by Country 85
4.4 Principals' External Accountability Toward Parents and School Management by Country 87
4.5 Teachers' and Principals' Accountability Toward Parents by Country 88
4.6 Teachers' and Principals' Accountability Toward School Management by Country 89
4.7 Teachers' Cultural Values by Country 91

4.8	Principals' Cultural Values by Country	92
4.9	Teachers' and Principals' Organizational Support by Country	99
5.1	Teachers' and Principals' Collectivism per Country in This Study and In-Group Collectivism Scores (Practice) From the GLOBE Project	139
5.2	Teachers' and Principals' External and Internal Accountability per Country in This Study and In-Group Collectivism Scores (Practice) From the GLOBE Project	141

Appendices

3.1	Handling of Missing Data	35
3.2	The Questionnaires Used in the Study (English Version)	36
3.3	Psychometric and Questionnaire Position of Study Variables	49
3.4	Check on Leveled Structure Teacher Data	51
3.5	Models for Teachers' Accountability	53
3.6	Models for Teachers' Accountability Toward Parents and School Management	63

Contributing chapter authors

Joris G.J. Beek is a PhD student in educational sciences at Utrecht University, the Netherlands. His research focuses on interest development and how interest development relates to adolescents' situatedness within their social practices. He has a teaching degree in mathematics, a bachelor's degree in pedagogical science, and a research master's degree in educational science. He has knowledge in advanced statistics such as multilevel analyses and social network analyses. Before becoming a PhD student, Joris worked as a researcher at Utrecht University and he was a mathematics and science teacher within pre-vocational education.

Chris Phielix, PhD, is an educational scientist and e-learning manager at the Faculty of Social and Behavioral Sciences at Utrecht University, the Netherlands. He is an experienced teacher in educational sciences and has knowledge and skills in designing (blended) learning modules. His research interests started with computer-supported collaborative learning (CSCL) and socio-emotional group behavior but expanded in recent years to research on teacher accountability and flipped learning. His research is published in international refereed journals.

Contributing researchers

Canada

Matthew Hurley has worked as a counselor, computer technician, science camp instructor, and as a child and youth worker. He is presently completing the final course in a graduate program in postsecondary education. His research interests include the relationship between student learning in on-campus courses as compared to online course offerings. Matthew is actively researching in the areas of postsecondary studies and teacher accountability.

Noel Hurley is Professor of Education and Chair of Graduate Programs in Leadership Studies at Memorial University, Newfoundland, Canada. His early research was concentrated in the area of educational finance and effective schools; he has broadened his research interests to include international comparative education, school effectiveness, and professional learning community practices. Noel has authored several refereed journal articles and government reports and has co-authored a leadership and head teacher training program that is being used in five West African countries. He has written one book, contributed chapters to several other books, and has presented more than 50 pieces of his research at peer-reviewed conferences.

China

Dandan Lu is a PhD candidate at the Faculty of Education, Memorial University, St. John's, Newfoundland and Labrador, Canada. She completed a master's thesis that investigated teacher perceptions toward teacher accountability in China. She is an experienced high school teacher at Xi'an Jiatong University High School.

Hungary

Nora Arato, PhD, has been a comparative and cross-cultural social science and education researcher in different departments at the University of Michigan (UM), USA. She has published and co-published on comparative education, juvenile crime, psychiatry, and different aspects of mixed method (qualitative and quantitative) research in medicine. As a senior research fellow at the Consortium of Cross-Cultural Research in Education (CCCRE) at the UM School of Education, she participated in four major cross-cultural and comparative research projects on change and accountability in teachers' and principals' work lives and contributed with several chapters to the consortium's publications while representing Hungary and the United States.

Zsolt Lavicza received his degrees in mathematics and physics in Hungary and then completed degrees in applied mathematics and mathematics education at the universities of Cincinnati and Michigan, USA, respectively. His PhD degree at the University of Cambridge focused on investigating issues in relation to the use of technologies in mathematics education. After completing his PhD, Zsolt taught educational research methodologies and mathematics education in Cambridge and other universities around the world. Currently, he is working on numerous research projects worldwide related to technology integration into schools; offering educational research training courses at a number of universities; leading a doctoral program in science, technology, engineering, and mathematics (STEM) education at Johannes Kepler University in Linz, Austria; and coordinating research projects within the International GeoGebra Institute.

The Netherlands

Perry den Brok is Professor and Chair of the Education and Learning Sciences group at Wageningen University and Research, the Netherlands. He is also chair of the 4TU Centre for Engineering Education, a center for educational innovation of the four universities of technology in the Netherlands (Twente, Delft, Eindhoven, and Wageningen). Perry was the European Editor of the *Learning Environments Research* journal for over ten years. Much of his research focuses on (perceptions of) the learning environment, including the role of teachers, but more recently he has focused on teacher professional learning and educational innovation, especially in the context of higher education. He publishes regularly on these topics in peer-reviewed journals, books, and book chapters and supervises several PhD students and postdocs on these topics.

South Africa and Zimbabwe

Johan Booyse is Professor Emeritus at the University of South Africa. From 1994 to 2003, he occupied a position as Head of the Departments of History of Education and Further Teacher Education, respectively. When he went into compulsory retirement at the end of 2017, he was a professor in the Department of Educational Foundations where he was responsible for providing tuition to postgraduate students in the fields of history of education, comparative education, and education management. He has published widely on themes related to both the system and the history of South African education.

Spain

Beatriz López has a degree in psychology and holds a University Expert certificate in the design and statistical treatment of surveys. Her research lines rest on the evaluation of the Spanish educational system, the quality of distance learning, and the study of gender and telecommunication and ICTs. Since 2007, she has been collaborating on several research projects of the Gender and Information Communication Technologies (ICT) research group at the Internet Interdisciplinary Institute of the Open University of Catalonia in Barcelona, Spain. She has published some of her collaborative work in international journals (e.g., *Sex Roles*) and book chapters in Spanish.

Julio Meneses, PhD, is Associate Professor of Research Methods in the Faculty of Psychology and Education of the Open University of Catalonia, Spain, and researcher at the Gender and Information Communication Technologies (ICT) research group of the Internet Interdisciplinary Institute. His current research interests lie in survey design and multivariate analysis, digital inequality, students' dropout and re-enrollment, and the use of technology by children and young people in and out of school. He teaches undergraduate and postgraduate courses on research methods, psychometrics, and statistics. He has published numerous journal articles in international outlets and is the author of books and book chapters in Spanish and Catalan.

Milagros Sáinz is currently the lead researcher of the Gender and Information Communication Technologies (ICT) research group at the Internet Interdisciplinary Institute of the Open University of Catalonia in Barcelona, Spain. Her research interests revolve around family and school influences on study choices; gender role development during adolescence; gender stereotypes about ability self-concepts, achievement, and task-choices; gendered construction of careers of occupations; and secondary school teachers' and students' attitudes toward technology and technological subjects. She has published numerous journal articles about all of these research issues in international journals as well as several books and book chapters in Spanish and Catalan.

Acknowledgments

The work reported in this book would not have been possible without the collaborative efforts of members of the Consortium for Cross-Cultural Research in Education (CCCRE). This consortium, which is associated with the American Educational Research Association (AERA), is home to an international research team that has been investigating various aspects of teachers' and principals' work over the past 30 years.[1] We are very grateful to the CCCRE founders – the late Al Menlo, the late Pam Poppleton, and Lee Collett, who led the consortium for more than 25 years and enabled the birth of the study on comparative accountability reported here.

As a long-time international team, the consortium's collaborative studies on teachers' and principals' work made us realize that many educational phenomena, including school accountability, were similar yet also different in our respective countries, being uniquely shaped by local national contexts and cultural values. The consortium members discussed issues and exchanged ideas related to accountability policy and educators' behavior in our respective countries. Our deliberations triggered questions about the nature of perceived accountability, its origins, supportive elements in its environment, the role of accountability audiences, and more. Given the increasing prominence of accountability regulation in teachers' and principals' work life in many countries, the consortium became interested in the systematic implications of culture and other contextual factors on the way educators perceive and experience work accountability. Because many publications on educational accountability seemed to originate in the U.S., our multi-country study was intended to balance readers' exposure to this phenomenon in different educational systems around the world.

Members of our team and consortium included Nora Arato (Hungary and the U.S.), Johan Booyse (South Africa and Zimbabwe), Noel Hurley (Canada), and Milagros Sáinz (Spain). We are profoundly indebted to them for their help in data collection and for their insights. This team was joined along the way by more researchers: Matthew Hurley (Canada), Zsolt

Lavicza (Hungary), Beatriz López (Spain), Dandan Lu (China), and Julio Meneses (Spain). We deeply appreciate the laborious work of these scholars in the data collection stage. Gonzalo Jover and Eduardo Garcia Jimenez kindly assisted in interpreting some of the Spanish results.

The elaborate methodological and statistical work needed for this study was performed in early stages by Perry den Brok and Chris Phielix (the Netherlands). Joris G.J. Beek (the Netherlands) was in charge of subsequent data processing and advanced statistical analyses.

Finally, we thank the teachers and principals who were so kind to complete our questionnaires.

Zehava Rosenblatt, University of Haifa, Israel
Theo Wubbels, Utrecht University, the Netherlands

Note

1 CCCRE publications: Menlo et al. (2015), Poppleton and Williamson (2004).

1 Introduction

The quest for accountability is almost as old as work itself. In Hall et al.'s (2017, p. 204) words, "accountability is a fundamental element of all societies and the organizations that operate within them." Accountability represents and defines basic social and economic relationships between participants to the point of representing social order. These relationships normally consist of one party taking responsibility for its own actions while the other party evaluates these actions and provides feedback. This basic accountability scheme is one of the foundations of human interaction, in particular in working scenes, and is the essence of the study offered in the present book.

This book is about the perceived facet of accountability in educational institutions, specifically schools. In educational institutions (as in many other organizations), accountability appears in two forms: the first is the system level, namely accountability that is attributed to organizations (schools) and is based on organizational structure and policy regulation, and the second form is the personal level, which is attributed to the individual (teacher, principal) and is based on individual characteristics. The focus of the current book is the second form, referred to by Hall et al. (2017) as "felt accountability." Felt accountability, according to these authors, is a state of mind, a subjective interpretation of a structured accountability context. We do not use the word 'felt' because personal-level accountability includes, as we see it, not only feelings but also cognitive perceptions. We refer to this concept as 'accountability disposition.'

As a subjective dispositional concept, accountability is likely to be influenced by myriad social forces that surround the individual. The present book focuses on cultural values as social forces that may explain differences in teachers' and principals' accountability dispositions in various contexts. In order to tap cultural effects, a multi-national study, consisting of eight countries from four continents, was launched in 2011, and its results are the basis for our book.

Two concerns drove the conception of this book. One was a steadily growing preoccupation among educational practitioners in recent decades with educational accountability as an answer to plummeting students' academic achievements. The second was a lacuna in current academic and practical literature (mainly originating from the U.S.) on conceptualization of the subjective accountability aspect in education. This lacuna apparently led to an emerging need for rigorous global research on accountability antecedents on the individual level. The coming together of these concerns produced the present book on accountability and culture in education.

Preoccupation with educational accountability as a panacea for educational ills

Widespread preoccupation with educational accountability has often been an issue among educators in many countries around the world (e.g., Easley & Tulowitzki, 2016; Müller & Hernández, 2010). One of the purest forms of system-wide accountability seems to be the U.S. policy titled *No Child Left Behind* (NCLB) that was conceived as a response to ongoing dissatisfaction with American students' poor academic outcomes (National Commission on Excellence in Education, 1983). The NCLB policy reflected the idea that educators' accountability for academic results would enhance students' grades and other academic outcomes through mechanisms such as evidence-based practice, standardized testing, imposition of performance standards, and feedback expressed by rewards as well as sanctions. The NCLB Act represented a pure accountability flagship model. It meant that schools had to report to the government about their performance based on clear standards. Schools that met these standards enjoyed governmental resources, while those that did not meet them faced sanctions such as principal dismissal and school closure. The *Every Student Succeeds Act* (ESSA, 2015) that followed the NCLB was more moderate in its rewards and sanctions, but the original essential accountability tenets remained intact.

At the same time, other countries around the world have adopted the accountability concept and developed various ways to embrace it in national educational systems. Easley and Tulowitzki (2016) showed, in a series of case studies, how accountability policy influenced school leadership in various countries. Their descriptions of accountability policies in 12 countries showed the great diversity of ways educators confront and cope with accountability demands, as well as similarities among countries. Müller

Introduction 3

and Hernández (2010) also underscored social processes that explained the nature of accountability policy in different countries. In a number of these country accounts, authors pointed to accountability policy that was based on bureaucratic regulations as problematic.

Along this line, soon after NCLB began the initial enthusiasm with accountability, theory and practice turned into widespread disenchantment with the policy results. Although some studies pointed to academic improvement in certain schools, as promised (Rosenblatt & Shimoni, 2002), others raised considerable concerns about neo-liberal currents that carried the drive toward accountability into questionable practices and pedagogic values (Ambrosio, 2013). Detrimental implications about educators' work, such as reduction in scope of teaching, social injustice, and intense pressure on principals and teachers started to emerge. Changing the formal American policy from NCLB to ESSA, indeed, reflected relaxation of rigid regulatory principles but did not dramatically change the inherent pressure on educators that accountability policies entailed.

The perturbing reports about educators' reactions to system accountability undoubtedly attested to the detrimental role the formal accountability approach and related mechanisms played in educators' work life and welfare. However, they also reflected the view that while educational decision makers were active participants, educational practitioners were left with a passive role in the accountability school operation. There are relatively few reports on accountability being rooted in the professional make-up of school educators. This is perhaps a reason why the substantial literature on system-level accountability generally ignored input of teachers' and principals' genuine accountability.

Naturally, teachers and principals are at the heart of the significant debate about and practice of accountability. Teachers are expected to be accountable for their students' achievements. Accordingly, teachers' work is closely monitored, and their performance is often rigorously recorded and evaluated. Erroneously and often paradoxically, these measures tend to affect teachers with work stress and resentment (Valli & Buese, 2007), reducing their autonomy, and furthering a tendency to teach only what is being evaluated (Ambrosio, 2013; Cochran-Smith et al., 2018; Darling-Hammond, 2007; Knapp & Feldman, 2012; Lee & Wong, 2004; Seashore-Louis et al., 2005). Similarly, principals, as heads of their respective schools, are individually targeted when their school's performance is challenged. They are held accountable for their school's academic success and failure (Firestone & Shipps, 2005). Principal failure may result in personal consequences, such as probation and dismissal, as specified in the NCLB and ESSA.

Surprisingly, despite the proliferation of literature on school accountability in general, and the effect of accountability on educators' work in particular, little attention has been paid to date to educators' individual accountability, namely, their inclination to feel accountable for their work in connection with accountability policy and professional codes. The present book is an effort to fill this void. Because of the importance of understanding the factors leading to a disposition for accountability vis-à-vis the relatively little academic knowledge on individual-level accountability, we set out in this book to specifically explore the relationship of cultural values with educators' accountability disposition.

Development of accountability theory

The theory of accountability as a subjective – perceived – concept is slowly growing. Early studies used labs or field experiments to investigate the effect of accountability on human behavior and cognition (Lerner & Tetlock, 1999; Tetlock, 1983). Studies generally found that the behavior of accountable employees was aimed at producing favorable outcomes among their audiences (Frink & Klimoski, 1998). It was also found that audience background, such as gender, affected employees' accountability behavior (Brandts & Garofalo, 2012). In education, a field-experiment study on the effect of teacher accountability showed that accountable teachers (measured by report/feedback relations with their superintendent) were more favorably evaluated by their respective principals than non-accountable teachers (Rosenblatt & Shimoni, 2002). Results of these studies showed consistently that accountability behavior and consequences were contingent on individuals' differences.

In the present study, we took these studies one step further to explore social antecedents of accountability. We leaned on Gelfand et al. (2004), who drew attention to the *cultural* perspective of accountability in organizations. These authors argued that accountability was expressed more strongly in individualist than collectivist societies. Similarly, Velayutham and Perera (2004) showed how the societal values of individualism and collectivism led to different levels of accountability based on emotional states (guilt and shame). Drawing from the vast body of knowledge on the effect of cultural values generally and individualism and collectivism specifically on organizational behavior (Gelfand et al., 2007), we set out to explore the relations of these two cultural values to accountability in education using a comparative cross-cultural approach.

This book is the result of a collaborative effort of researchers in the Consortium for Cross-Cultural Research in Education. They met each other through participating in international conferences and represent eight countries: Canada, China, Hungary, Israel, the Netherlands, South Africa, Spain, and Zimbabwe. Based on the theoretical background (Chapter 2), we outline our research methods (Chapter 3) and describe our cross-country findings (Chapter 4). In Chapter 5, we discuss and interpret our results and then conclude with our thoughts and observations about the theoretical and practical implications of our study (Chapter 6).

2 Teachers' and principals' accountability
Theoretical background

The social and psychological theories on which the present study is based range across topics that seem to be basic to the understanding of perceived accountability in education. Our research model is focused on cultural values (collectivism and individualism) as major predictors of accountability. In addition, we have also investigated the added contribution of perceived organizational support. Surprisingly, unlike the rich bibliographical background on cultural values and organizational support, literature on accountability as a personal disposition is relatively scant. In this chapter, we start with conceptualizing perceived accountability in education, focusing on accountability dimensionality and selected accountability audiences and describing the way accountability was measured in the present study. Then we proceed to present the predictors advanced by this study – collectivism, individualism on both individual and country levels, and perceived organizational support.

Conceptualizing accountability

Accountability: definition and foundations

Applied to work behavior, accountability has been the focus of a relatively small but persistent body of research, including early studies that tried to capture the essence of this particular phenomenon. For example, Frink and Ferris (1998, p. 1260) viewed accountability as "a system of review of behavior by some constituency, with substantial rewards or punishments being contingent on the review." Another early definition stated that accountability is the "implicit or explicit expectation that one may be called on to justify one's beliefs, feelings, and actions to others" (Lerner & Tetlock, 1999, p. 255). A decade later, Hall et al. (2009, p. 381) defined accountability as "holding people answerable for their decisions and actions." Soon after, Hall and Ferris (2011, p. 134) defined accountability as a "perceived expectation that one's decisions or actions will be evaluated by a salient audience and that rewards or sanctions are believed to be contingent on this expected evaluation."

These definitions focused on accountability as a concrete organizational phenomenon, characterized by the interaction of two parties that are often referred to as *agent* and *audience*. The agent is expected to report on his/her work conduct and to justify it, whereas the audience responds with a performance evaluation, direct feedback, and sometimes rewards or sanctions. These relations are based on clear formal and informal work standards that are shared and agreed upon by the two parties. In education, typical dyads of this sort would be teacher-principal and principal-educational board, while many other dyads, to various degrees of formality, are possible.

Accountability agents should meet the following three stipulations: *responsibility, transparency*, and *answerability* (Drach-Zahavi et al., 2018). Responsibility is sometimes used as a synonymous term to accountability. For example, in the Merriam-Webster Dictionary (Laird, 1971), accountability is defined as "an obligation or willingness to accept responsibility or to account for one's actions." Largely, responsibility involves an inner commitment to one's obligations within the accountability framework. Transparency alludes to work morality and ethics. Effective and accurate accountability would necessarily assume an honest work report on the agent's part, as well as an impartial evaluation from the audience in response. Answerability refers to the agent's obligation to be constantly ready to report on his or her own deeds – the work process as well as work results. The three elements together represent the work values behind the agent's accountability to any given audience.

Although responsibility, transparency, and answerability are at the heart of the agent's report, still, the way the report is transmitted may be erroneously contingent on work results. Authors (e.g., Hareli et al., 2005; Shaw et al., 2003) showed that when work performance did not meet standards, agents turned to defensive tactics intended to reduce the severity of the performance outcome (justification), reduce responsibility (excuses), accept both the responsibility and undesirability of the situation (concession), or reject both (denial). Teachers, then, in their report to school management may attribute their students' academic failures to the work of other colleagues or to poor working conditions. Principals may also use 'impression management' tactics (Frink & Ferris, 1998) in their report to school boards and attribute school failure to the inadequacy of faculty training or a lack of resources.

To be a relevant accountability audience, two requirements have to be met: *legitimacy* and *entitlement*. Legitimacy is met when the agent is convinced that the audience has a formal right to get the work report and to act upon it. A fundamental example in education would be a school principal who has an *ex-officio* right to receive the work report from his or her faculty member. Entitlement is met when the agent perceives the audience to possess a natural right to receive the report. For example, teachers' accountability to parents would be contingent on the degree to which parents are perceived by teachers as possessing the natural right to receive reports regarding their respective children's academic achievements and behavior (see more on parents as an accountability audience later). While agents expect audiences to be legitimate and entitled, audiences also have expectations about agents' conduct and sincerity.

The accountability exchange between the agent and the audience is based, as mentioned earlier, on clear standards and work goals, ideally agreed upon and shared between parties. As goal orientation is about one's motivation to achieve and attain favorable evaluations and invest in learning and development (Heintz & Steele-Johnson, 2004), it seems a solid foundation for an effective discourse between the two respective accountability parties. Accepting standards and aspiring to meet goals constitutes an inherent part of the accountability scene, and is a key to interpreting its outcomes. The concept of goal aspiration, then, helps us to understand how goal-oriented agents adhere to accountability rules while developing professionally.

In sum, the key elements in a two-party accountability relationship are shared goals and work standards, responsibility and answerability in the form of transparent performance reports, audience legitimacy and entitlement, performance evaluation, feedback, and rewards and/or sanctions. These elements work in concert so that shared goals dictate the nature of the work report, followed by work assessment, respective feedback, and subsequent rewards and sanctions. This sequence is subject to changes in working goals, agent dispositions and motivation, organizational policy, and audience characteristics.

This complex model of accountability may appear in different levels of analysis. As mentioned in the introductory chapter of this book, accountability in education is most evident on a system level, where the agent is typically the school (normally represented by the principal) and the audience is correspondingly the government, local educational administration, or private educational enterprise. Accountability in education appears also at the individual level, where the agent is typically the teacher or the principal and the audience is any supervisory party (the principal in the case of teachers and the school board in the case of principals). Both system and individual accountability, when framed formally and bureaucratically, may be termed '*objective accountability.*' The present study deals with accountability at the individual level from a *subjective* point of view, as described next.

Accountability as a subjective concept

The relatively limited amount of literature on accountability as a subjective concept is puzzling because it is hard to imagine human compliance with formal rules of accountability without personal involvement consisting of subjective interpretation, motivation, inclinations, and feelings toward such rules. This is the basic rationale and prime tenet of the present study. The personal aspect of system accountability may be termed '*subjective accountability*' because it consists of the way accountability is perceived by the individual and accordingly employs self-report measures.

The subjective aspect of accountability reflects one's genuine desire to be accountable for one's own work performance and outcomes, including the wish to follow accountability guidelines. It is the way one makes sense of institutional accountability policy and context vis-à-vis one's own standards of conduct. An example and illustration of subjective accountability in nursing was offered by Leonenko and Drach-Zahavy (2016). These authors defined nurses' personal accountability in the following way: "the value of accountability serves as a moral compass guiding behavior" (p. 165). Applied to education, we believe that teachers and principals perceive accountability as a professional and moral experience that complements and corresponds with a formal accountability context.

The notion of "felt-accountability," referred to by Hall et al. (2017) and introduced by Hochwarter et al. (2005) and Schlenker and Weigold (1989), represents another conceptualization of the subjective facet of accountability. Felt accountability pertains to the personal helping mechanisms of perceiving and acting in line with accountability. These mechanisms provide inner standards and goals that direct the individual in the way that accountability relations should be conducted.

Manifestations of accountability in educational institutions have been roughly classified by a few authors into two types: *external* and *internal*. Because subjective accountability may be evoked by either outside triggers (institutional expectations) or inner drives (professional calling), we will apply this two-way classification to describe two dimensions of subjective accountability.

Accountability dimensions: external and internal

Firestone and Shipps (2005) offered a two-way conceptualization of school administrators' accountability: external and internal. External accountability, according to these authors, refers to a situation where the agent reports to bodies that are *different than the self*, for example teachers reporting to their respective principals or principals reporting to review boards. This accountability type would reflect the agent's response to formal regulations regarding educational accountability. The focus of this accountability type is on *outer* expectations that have to be met by the school educators. External accountability, according to these authors, typically operates in three educational arenas: bureaucratic (school procedures, governmental regulations), political (citizen pressures, legal mandates), and market (competition among educational institutions). Although external accountability, as conceptualized by Firestone and Shipps (2005), was intended to describe school administrators' accountability, this theoretical framework can be applied to teachers as well. In the teachers' case, the bureaucratic arena would be the school principal, political audiences would be parents or fellow teacher-colleagues, and the market arena may be exemplified by new and popular educational methods. Fullan et al. (2015, p. 4) refer to external accountability with the following words: "when system leaders measure the public through transparency, monitoring and selective intervention that their system is performing in line with social expectations and requirements."

The other accountability dimension suggested by Firestone and Shipps (2005) was labeled internal and consists of educators' *inner* commitment to professional standards, such as good work practices and personal moral beliefs. Apparently, the agent and the audience in the internal case are identical, where the agent 'reports' to his or her own values and ethical codes. Knapp and Feldman (2012, p. 669), who adopted Firestone and Shipps' (2005) external-internal classification, described internal accountability in the following way:

> Individuals in the school have expectations for themselves and often for others, and those expectations are demonstrated and discerned in the instructional decisions educators make, their descriptions of their work, and their interactions with each other . . . individual teachers are left to hold themselves to account for successfully educating the students in their charge.

Similarly, Fullan et al. (2015, p. 4) argued that internal accountability occurs "when individuals and groups willingly take on personal, professional and collective responsibility for continuous improvement and success for all students." Internal accountability, then, does not follow any formal standards; rather it adheres to inner professional principles.

In a multiple case study of U.K. teachers undergoing educational reform, Poulson (1998) also distinguished two aspects of teacher accountability. The first was external, operating through contractual obligation and inspection, and the second was internal, representing 'self-regulation,' where teachers were responsible to themselves as professionals and defined their accountability in terms of moral education. Likewise, Eraut (1993) conceptualized teacher professionalism as including a moral commitment to serve in the students' interests and having a feeling of obligation "to develop one's practical knowledge both by personal reflection and through interaction with others" (p. 28). This description underscores internal accountability in a professional framework. The two-way classification of accountability dimensionality then is generally consistent among the authors mentioned here.

The central foundations of internal accountability are work ethic and professionalism. Work ethic represents an aggregation of beliefs about one's work behavior (Miller et al., 2002; Petty & Hill, 1995) focused on *morality* and *hard work*. Both concepts – morality and hard work – seem to be major tenets of accountability. High morality, or what Oser (1991) refers to as high teacher *ethos*, is essential to the teacher's succinct report of achievements as well as failures in work. Morality would help to neutralize the employee's often recorded tendency to manage the impressions others have of his or her work (Dubrin, 2011). Hard work would also characterize sound accountability relations, when the teacher or principal strives to comply with regulatory guidelines or follow their inner professional inclinations. Another way to express the relations between accountability and ethics was offered by Dubnick's (2003) essay on the ethics of accountability. This author argued that ethics have often been associated with standards of responsible behavior and professional integrity. This association is based, according to the author, on answerability, blameworthiness, liability, and attributability, all intended to shape the way performance report is perceived by the key audiences.

Professionalism is another tenet of internal accountability. Sugrue and Sefika (2017) discussed *professional responsibility* as a response to harsh 'accountability language' (referring to bureaucratic accountability). They described professional responsibility as

> a sense of calling to provide service for the benefit of others, . . . being morally responsible for one's behavior; to take on important duties while being willing to make independent decisions. . . . It connotes both the personal and moral dimensions of having a commitment to care.
> (Sugrue and Sefika, 2017, p. 174)

This idea of professional responsibility is therefore close in meaning to the internal dimension of accountability, as conceptualized by previous authors (Firestone & Shipps, 2005; Knapp & Feldman, 2012; Poulson, 1998) and adopted in the present study. Professional responsibility, according to Sugrue and Sefika (2017), stands in contrast to accountability in its objective sense, the latter characterized by control rather than trust, and relies on compliance and conformity to a set of predetermined measures or outcomes.

The notion of control may be used to further demonstrate the difference between external and internal accountability. As stated by Dubnick (2003, p. 405) in his essay on ethics and accountability: "accountability has traditionally been regarded as the means used to control and direct administrative behavior." External accountability represents control that comes from the outside, typically from superiors who have the power to exert administrative measures that either reward or punish. Internal accountability on the other hand reflects self-control that derives from one's own moral power.

Finally, although the two accountability dimensions have been presented here as two distinct concepts, both dimensions seem to be interconnected to a great extent. Dubnick (2003) argued that ethical behavior is inseparable from external accountability. In response to the question of whether or not accountability fosters ethical behavior, Dubnick (2003) maintained that different accountability facets call for compatible ethical strategies. For example, accountability characterized by blameworthiness will need higher moral standards, while attributability-driven accountability calls for citizenship ethics, implying higher standards of personal conduct.

Accountability audiences

The accountability audience – its legitimacy and particularly its relations with the respective 'agent' (teacher, principal) – is one of the central topics in the present study. The audience in accountability interaction is the party that receives the agent's work report and responds to it. Because accountability is treated here as an individual disposition, the obvious key to understand this concept is one's psychological make-up. However, given the bipartisan context of one's accountability at work, it is conceivable that the nature of the receiving party – the audience – contributes to the understanding of accountability as well. Moreover, as in every organization, schools consist of a number of potential audiences (e.g., the school management team, students, parents, supporting staff, educational board, local education authority) where each potentially expects a report on school outcomes. Therefore, the study of personal accountability would not be complete without the understanding of the nature and effect of the accountability audience.

A convenient theoretical framework to understand the audience role in the accountability agent-audience interrelation is the Stakeholder Theory (Freeman et al., 2010). This theory states that organizations are populated by diverse parties of different natures, while all share an interest in the organization's success. School effectiveness, according to this theory, would depend on bringing together the disparate interests of these stakeholders, rather than focusing on one seemingly most influential party. A practical example to this assertion in a school context was offered by Bibu and Saris (2017), who studied Arab schools in Israel. They showed empirically how schools' successful operations were dependent on principals' ability to put together the different stakeholders' concerns and desires.

Of all typical school stakeholders, two seem to be the most relevant accountability audiences, although very different in nature: *school management* and *parents*. School management is the most legitimate and entitled audience for both teachers and principals. Similar to any other organization, reporting to management on work processes and outcomes is a basic formal standard act in the organization's operations. The typical cycle for accountability (work report, feedback, work assessment, and related rewards) is mandatory in regard to superiors. Looking through subjective lenses, teachers may be personally invested in both bureaucratic (external) and professional (internal) accountability, being inherently interested in receiving feedback and subsequent managerial actions, such as enhanced professional training and promotion. Teachers are likely to believe that the very essence of a voluntary work report increases the chances to be favorably evaluated and positively rewarded. Principals may also be subjectively interested in reporting on their managerial work as a way to justify decisions and actions and get board approval for managerial decisions and actions.

When parents are considered stakeholders, external accountability from both teachers and principals is not as obvious as in the case of school management. First, parents' status in schools is minimal – they are obviously part of school context but at the same time formally external to it (Addi-Raccah & Friedman, 2019). Parents' status is somewhat vague compared to other potential school stakeholders such as teachers, principals, and students themselves. Indeed, parents' relevancy to children's education is not questioned, considering their familial attachment to their children and their legal parental guardianship. Certainly, parents are deeply interested in the nature of the academic and social education their children receive in schools. More broadly, the neo-liberal approach to education promotes the idea of parental responsibility and active involvement in schools as potential clients (Vincent & Ball, 2006). Consequently, parents are increasingly demanding and expecting more answers and explanations for school processes and outcomes.

However, teachers tend to be reluctant to allow parents to step into their educational territory. Parental involvement is often viewed by teachers as interfering with their professional practice (Egger et al., 2015), in particular considering parents' lack of formal educational training. Teachers believe that accepting the presence of parents in the school educational scene would legitimize the parental assessment and criticism of teachers' work (Bæck, 2010). As teaching is classified as a semi-professional occupation, teachers are constantly striving to extend their training, education, and credentials. To enhance their professional status, teachers seek to draw a clear division of labor between themselves as professionals and parents as laypeople (Addi-Raccah & Grinshtain, 2018). In addition, the heavy workload is also mentioned as a major reason for teachers to rebuff parental involvement (Anastasiou & Papagianni, 2020). For these reasons, teachers' relations with parents are elusive and controversial; while a professional code should motivate teachers to collaborate with parents, perceived professional image and work hardship may make them push parents away from core educational work.

Although principals' approach to parental involvement may be similar to that of teachers, it would be more typical for principals to deal with parents as a formal collective group (e.g., a school parents' organization or a local chapter of a national parents-teachers' association) than as individuals. In any case, principals also see parents as unique stakeholders with whom relations are controversial, based on the way parents' unofficial influence is perceived (Sezgin-Nartgün, 2017). In terms of policy, parental involvement in schools should be welcomed by principals who are continuously reaching out for external resources. Parental social impact, in particular among parents with high social-economic status, may be considerable. Sezgin-Nartgün (2017) reported that both principals and vice-principals in Turkish schools considered parents as the largest source of non-formal influence in their respective schools. The sources of parental impact derive from parents' occupational and academic backgrounds, as well as their genuine interest in assisting the school to advance academically and socially. Using this influence, parents can help principals in leading and mobilizing educational changes. As Scott and Halkias (2016) showed, collaboration with parents is important to sound educational policy and successful leadership.

Ironically, when parents have high social-economic status, their identification with school goals does not guarantee acceptance of parents' ideas and collaboration between principals and parents. Principals may draw away from parental involvement and see it as a potential threat to their managerial discretion, thus creating a source of conflict (Lareau & Muñoz, 2012). In other words, the informal power of school parents can be viewed as a double-edged sword. The way principals cope with this dichotomy can be explained using the Impression Management Theory (Dubrin, 2011), which describes people's attempt to influence the way other people perceive them or interpret organizational results (Conway et al., 2015; Frink & Ferris, 1998). Borrowed from general management literature, this theory was also applied to school administration. Gardner and Martinko (1988) studied the impression management strategies of school administrators and showed that principals presented themselves differently to disparate types of audiences. Self-presentation is advanced by influence tactics shaped by the estimation of the stakeholder's potential influence on the organization. In their study, Gardner and Martinko (1988) showed that school principals targeted superiors as preferred audiences over other stakeholders, such as school parents, using verbal self-presentation as an influential tactic. These studies attest to clear discrimination of both teachers and principals in their relations with different school stakeholders, affecting these educators' accountability to the two audiences discussed – school management and parents.

Accountability differences among audiences raise the following question: to what extent is accountability a stable personal disposition, or does it vary according to audience context? Several authors (e.g., Staw et al., 1986; Staw & Ross, 1985) argued that individual dispositions at work (such as job satisfaction) tended to be a considerably stable source over time. Davis-Blake and Pfeffer (1989) went one step further and showed that stable dispositional job attitudes were affected by non-dispositional causes that may have been embedded in individual attributes (e.g., race) but also in situational attributes such as the social network in which the individual operates. Social networks in schools consist of various players (stakeholders), of which school management and parents are particularly conspicuous. In sum, it seems that both dispositional and situational approaches to accountability dispositions are entangled, and this entanglement best explains teachers' and principals' complex accountability to school audiences.

Accountability measurement

Early studies on the effect of accountability on employees' behavior and cognitions used laboratory and field study methods. In lab experiments, respondents were typically led to believe that their goals and achievements would be evaluated by 'supervisors' (Roch & McNall, 2007; Tetlock, 1992; Tetlock & Boettger, 1994). In field experiments, accountability was inferred from real performance monitoring and supervisors' feedback (e.g., Frink & Ferris, 1998). In education, Rosenblatt and Shimoni (2002) conducted a year-long field experiment, where physical education (PE) teachers reported on their work achievements to their PE superintendent and received the superintendent's feedback and work evaluation in return.

These lab and field experimental studies used objective accountability measures, such as observations of the agent's report or (in Rosenblatt & Shimoni's 2002 study) reports submitted to a superior (superintendent). In order to learn about variation in educators' approach and internal feelings in regard to organizational accountability expectations, self-report measures may be used. Such measures could also enable prediction analyses of accountability by personal attributes. Accordingly, scholars called for the need to explore the subjective experience of accountability (Hall et al., 2007).

In response to this call, a few self-report accountability scales were developed and tailored to specific sectors such as nursing (Drach-Zahavi et al., 2018), general industry (Ferris et al., 1997; Thoms et al., 2002), managers (Wood & Winston, 2007), and adult students (Frink & Ferris, 1998; Hochwarter et al., 2005). The measures used in these studies were not consistent in their conceptualization of accountability. In a thorough review of self-report measures, Drach-Zahavi et al. (2018) argued that most measures failed to cover a full content domain of the accountability concept.

The present study employed Rosenblatt's (2017) accountability scale, based on Firestone and Shipps' (2005) two-way classification of school administrators' accountability, and adapted it to teachers. The scale included external accountability, referring to one's 'reporting' relations with bodies other than self (e.g., principal, school management, parents), and internal accountability, referring to 'reporting' to self (professional and ethical values). The three accountability attributes mentioned earlier – responsibility, transparency, and answerability – were also reflected in the scale (for further details please see Chapter 3 – Study Methods – and for the full scale see Appendix 3.2).

Accountability and cultural values

Cultural values and organizational behavior

As mentioned in the introduction to this book, there has been a widespread preoccupation with educational accountability among educators in many countries around the world in recent years (Easley & Tulowitzki, 2016). Global educational changes and widespread educators' preoccupation with school accountability inspired the present research to explore cultural antecedents of educational accountability based both on individual and country differences in cultural values. Cultural values have become a focus of rigorous cross-country research, starting with Hofstede's (1983) seminal research from around the globe. Subsequent research on organizational behavior provided abundant evidence for the effect of cultural values on employees' work behavior (e.g., Gelfand et al., 2007). Results repeatedly showed that cultural values could explain individuals' differences on various issues (e.g., organizational leadership [House et al., 2004]). More specifically, employees' organizational behaviors may depend on the cultural values to which they adhere, that in turn may depend on the values prominent in their community or country.

To understand the relationships among societal cultures, individuals' cultural values, and accountability as work behavior we need to focus on Erez and Earley's (1993) Theory of Culture and Self-Identity at work. They suggested that societal cultural values have an important effect on how the self interprets stimuli. They argued that when significant others surrounding the focal individual share the same value system and behavioral norms, the individual's self would be modified by the culture. A modified self-concept would then be the means linking cultural beliefs with emergent work behaviors. Erez and Earley's (1993) conceptualization was applied here to work accountability, focusing on two cultural values: individualism and collectivism. These two values were selected based on Triandis (1980, 2001), who asserted that individualism and collectivism were the most important concepts needed to understand human values from a cultural perspective and that these values characterized the cultural make-up of communities.

Cultural values: individualism and collectivism

Individualism and collectivism refer to the nature of the relationship between the individual and the group and can be defined as the degree to which individuals are supposed to look after themselves or, alternatively, remain integrated into groups or families. Individualism reflects adherence to personal aspirations, autonomy, freedom, independence, and achievement orientation (Schwartz, 1994; Triandis, 1995). Individualistic employees would give priority to their own motivation and interests over those of the group, unlike collectivistic employees who would give preference to their group's interests. Collectivistic behavior, thoughts, and feelings are typically determined by the groups' norms (Markus & Kitayama, 1991). Both individualism and collectivism are expressed in employees' organizational behavior, and were proved to predict a wide range of work attitudes and behaviors (Gelfand et al., 2007).

Applied to education, a number of studies found links between the two values and teachers' attitudes and behaviors in school. For example, Teo and Huang (2019) showed that collectivism was positively related to the tendency of Chinese pre-service teachers to use new technology at work. In Ghana, teachers' collectivism was associated with the belief in restorative justice (Parimah et al., 2018). In a four-country study, Jiang (2016) showed that teachers' attribution of low socio-economic status to students' failures was different in collectivistic countries (Hong Kong, Singapore, and Taiwan, where personal factors were attached to academic failure) than in an individualistic country (the U.S., where situational factors were emphasized). A study conducted in Turkey showed that teachers' individualism and collectivism were related to their views on school functions and missions (Yilmaz et al., 2016). These studies in various countries clearly illustrated the potential role of individualism and collectivism in understanding educators' attitudes and behavior in schools.

To further understand individualistic and collectivistic expression in society, Triandis (2001) introduced the concept of society hierarchy. Accordingly, he divided individualism and collectivism into two sub-dimensions: vertical and horizontal. While the horizontal dimension referred to a non-hierarchical society, where everybody is like everybody else, the vertical dimension referred to a hierarchical society, where the self is different than the other self (see also Triandis & Gelfand, 1998). For the eight countries participating in the present study (seven democracies, one post-communist), the horizontal dimension seemed to be the most appropriate as a standard.

Relations between individualism and collectivism were another issue that had to be resolved in the present study. Traditionally, the two values were considered to be on opposite ends of one conceptual continuum, stretching from individualism to collectivism (e.g., Hofstede, 1983; House et al., 2004). According to this view, high collectivism would necessarily mean that individualism is low, and vice versa. Triandis (1993) argued that although collectivism and individualism appeared to be opposites in several country-focused studies, these values still often coexisted separately and each was simply "emphasized more or less in a given culture, depending on the situation" (p. 162). Later studies supported this argument and showed that collectivism and individualism certainly did not appear to be opposites in one dimension (Triandis, 2004; Watson & Morris, 2002) but rather did behave as two independent variables. We have adopted this view and included both separate variables in our study with regards to accountability.

Finally, the unit of analysis is an important issue to consider in culture-related studies. Although cultural values have typically and historically characterized societies, research increasingly showed, as mentioned earlier, that they can describe individual differences (Erez & Earley, 1993; Triandis & Suh, 2002) as well. The current study refers mostly to the individual level of analysis, but we also present and discuss the society (country, in our case) level.

Accountability and its relationship to individualism and collectivism

The link between cultural values and accountability was thoroughly conceptualized by Gelfand et al. (2004). These authors posited that a cultural perspective on accountability in organizations is critical for both theoretical and practical reasons. Theoretically, they claimed that accountability systems vary according to cultural values, as organizational functioning has culture-specific aspects. Using cultural values, employees create 'cognitive maps' to decipher accountability webs in their organizations. These 'maps' help employees navigate through organizational expectations.

All cultures have accountability systems to create predictability, order, and control, and the nature of such systems is highly culture specific (Gelfand & Realo, 1999). The relationship between cultural values and accountability was phrased by Gelfand et al. (2004, p. 137) in the following way:

> Individuals in different cultures are educated to understand the unique expectations that exist at different levels in the social system, the strength of these expectations, and the consequences for deviations from these expectations... thus, we argue that as individuals are enculturated through socialization in a particular sociocultural context, they develop ideas of how various individuals, groups, and organizations are answerable or accountable to one another.

It follows that the level of school educators' accountability disposition may vary in accordance with individuals' cultural perceptions. We may expect then that educators' accountability dispositions would be related to the degree that individuals adhere to individualistic or collectivistic values.

Gelfand et al. (2004) further specified the way accountability is expressed in individualistic and collectivistic societies. In individualistic cultures, accountability generally rests with specific individuals. Because the individual is motivated and led by his or her own personal aspirations and inclinations, results are attributed to the focal individual. In collectivistic cultures, group members tend to share rewards as well as repercussions resulting from common work, and consequently accountability would rest with the entire group; the group is primarily culpable and individuals are not necessarily identified. Thus, in individualistic societies individuals are held accountable for achieving results whereas in collectivistic societies groups are made accountable. This argument is in line with the fact that in individualistic societies individuals are the ones to be evaluated whereas in collectivistic societies group performance is mainly assessed.

The nature of relations between accountability disposition and cultural values is also addressed by Velayutham and Perera (2004), who studied human feelings in the context of cultural values. These authors showed that societal values of individualism and collectivism may lead to different levels of accountability based on the emotional states of guilt and shame. Whereas guilt would be a leading accountability-related emotion in individualistic societies, shame seems more prominent in collectivistic cultures. They then argued that in cultures with high individualistic values, a relatively high degree of accountability prevails because of agents' feelings of guilt. In collectivistic cultures, where shame prevails, a lower degree of accountability would be found.

Applied to education, teachers' and principals' accountability will be shaped by the individualistic or collectivistic culture to which they adhere. Teachers will be held *personally* accountable in an individualistic culture, so that students' academic achievements, as individuals or classes, would be attributed to the respective teachers – their qualifications, work effort, and capabilities. In a collectivistic culture, teachers would perceive their accountability as shared with other school faculty members. The group (teacher faculty, work team) then would mediate the connection of the individual to the organization in collectivistic societies. In sum, one could expect that the more teachers adhere to individualistic values, the more they feel personally accountable. Conversely, the more they stick to collectivistic values, the less they would feel personally accountable.

Regarding school principals, their accountability, as related to individualism and collectivism, seems to be different than that of teachers. Similar to teachers, principals are perceived as individuals who are personally responsible for their respective schools' performance. However, principals are also viewed as school symbols, being the representatives of the institutions they head and thus responsible for any schools' outcomes. Therefore, principals are typically held as primarily accountable to school management boards and local or governmental educational authorities. Grinshtain and Gibton (2018), who studied Israeli school principals, pointed to a gap between principals' responsibility vis-à-vis accountability regulations and their experience of relatively low authority and power. Given these circumstances, we would expect, then, that principals would tend to feel *personally accountable* in any cultural milieu, individualistic or collectivistic.

For both teachers and principals, we expect specific relations between the two cultural values and the two accountability dimensions – external and internal. This expectation draws from Gelfand et al.'s (2004, p. 145) assertion about 'self-accountability' with reference to cultural values. In their words:

> Over time, with the emphasis on individual standards that is cultivated in socialization and education in individualistic cultures . . . coupled with the lack of contextual standards (e.g., group standards), individuals are attuned to evaluate their own actions and deviations from their own standards.

Following these authors, we speculate that adherence to individualistic standards leads to accountability that is based more on inner guidance rather than on institutional or group standards, namely, more on the internal than the external dimension.

Using Erez and Earley's (1993) conceptualization, internal accountability is derived from one's need to be positively evaluated by one's own professional standards (individualistic norms). This would imply that in individualistic cultures we could expect teachers and principals to have higher internal than external accountability dispositions. As for external accountability, it would likely be related to collectivistic standards because members of work groups, as well as their supervisors, can clearly see, witness, and assess each member's contribution, even when end results (rewards and punishments) are at the group level (e.g., academic success of a class that is taught by more than one teacher). External accountability stems from the need to be evaluated by superiors and others in the working context (collectivistic norms). One's collectivistic values, therefore, may be more related to external than internal accountability.

In sum, we believe that individualism and collectivism may predict internal and external accountability. Our analyses, based on survey data taken from teachers and principals, explores these predictive relations in general and among specific school audiences. Given our multiple-country data base, we also look into societal cultural values, represented by our eight country samples, as specified next.

Accountability and country-level individualism and collectivism

The previous section dealt with relations of individual-level (teachers, principals) individualism and collectivism to accountability. Another way to examine associations between cultural values and accountability is to look at the accountability values of different countries. The country can be regarded as an overarching cultural entity, representing the aggregate comprised of preferences, values, and behavioral tendencies of people who share bordered living areas (including cultural segregation and subcultures). Several studies have shown that cultural values aggregated over country inhabitants differ between countries (e.g., Hofstede, 2011; House et al., 2004). Consistent with our previous argument that individual cultural values relate to accountability, we maintain that aggregated country values are related to individuals' accountability as well. In other words, accountability dispositions, both external and internal, could be a product of society's or country's cultural fabric that collectively inspires people in their accountability approach.

Aggregated scores show quite distinct and consistent differences among countries, as evidenced by the results of the large-scale studies of House et al. (2004, 2014) and Hofstede (1983, 2010). Yet, the Hofstede methodology was criticized (e.g., Baskerville, 2003). Applying country-level cultural values was said to be limited because the within-country variance in cultural values is often much larger than the between-countries variability (e.g., Greenfield, 2014). Therefore, we cannot assume that peoples' individual level of adhering to cultural values is the same as the cultural values score of the country with which they are affiliated (e.g., Beugelsdijk & Welzel, 2018; Hofstede, 2011).

Based on this criticism, we have applied two strategies in the present study to characterize cultural values in our participating countries and have explored their predictive effect on teachers' and principals' accountability. One strategy was to aggregate the scores collected from our study respondents by country. This seemed to be the most direct country characterization of teachers and principals in our study, grouped in their national countries. The second strategy was to borrow House et al.'s (2014) results, which were based on data coming from very large samples of managers and leaders (not educators) from various organizations in 62 societies that included all eight countries participating in the present study. These data seemed to be largely representative of the respective countries' populations, thereby probably capturing the countries' cultural values. Using these data in our present study made up for the concern mentioned previously about potential within-country variance.

Expectations regarding the relationships between the degree of country individualism and collectivism and teachers' and principals' accountability dispositions can be derived from earlier research mentioned in the beginning of the section Accountability and Cultural Values. Based on authors such as Gelfand et al. (2004) and Velayutham and Perera (2004), we expected countries characterized by either collectivism or individualism to relate positively to teachers' and principals' accountability, where the relation with individualism would be stronger than that of collectivism.

Accountability and organizational support

Although the research model of the present study centered on cultural values as predictors of accountability disposition, we have also added organizational support as an additional predictor and potential moderator of relations between cultural values and accountability. The reasons for including this variable were its potential to predict employees' attitudes and behavior at work and its particular relevancy to work accountability.

Organizational support was conceptualized by Rhodes and Eisenberger (2002, p. 698) as "[t]he extent to which employees perceive that their contributions are valued by their organizations and that their firm cares about their well-being." The assumption here is that organizations vary by the importance they attach to caring about their employees, consideration of their various needs, and showing appreciation for employees' contributions to the organization. This variation implies that employees' perceptions of such organizational support varies, too. There is some evidence that the perceived organizational support varies across cultures (e.g., Meyers et al., 2019).

The possible effect of organizational approach on employees' conduct at work has been widely investigated by scholars since the early days of the theoretical development of this concept by Eisenberger et al. (1986). Numerous studies have investigated the relations between organizational support and organizational orientations, i.e., individual's predisposition toward work, motivation to work, job satisfaction, and ways of dealing with peers, subordinates, and supervisors on the job (see the review in Eisenberger et al., 2020). Generally, results have indicated that employees' work attitudes and behavior improved when organizations were perceived as catering to their needs. In education, studies have shown that organizational support was directly related to teachers' positive work orientations, such as organizational commitment (Bibi et al., 2019; Nataly et al., 2019), organizational citizenship behavior (Eisenberger et al., 2020; Nataly et al., 2019), job satisfaction (Bibi et al., 2019), intention to stay on the job (Aria et al., 2019), positive affect (Candra-Dewi & Riantoputra, 2019), and work performance (Farooqi et al., 2019).

This abundance of evidence of the association between perceived organizational support and a broad variety of desirable teachers' work attitudes and behaviors suggests that perceived organizational support may also be related to accountability disposition. Two studies focused on this association. In the first study, Wikhamn and Hall (2014) showed that while previous research failed to establish direct relations between felt accountability and job satisfaction, the inclusion of organizational support in the research models brought to light its role as a moderator of the relation between accountability and job satisfaction. In other words, felt accountability interacted with organizational support in its relation to job satisfaction. Thus, only when organizational support was part of the model's independent variables could the contribution of job satisfaction to accountability prediction be shown. In a later study, Candra-Dewi and Riantoputra (2019) presented a reverse model of the relations between organizational support and felt accountability. They showed that employees who perceived their organizations as supportive felt more accountable.

The link between perceived organizational support and positive work attitudes and behavior may be interpreted using the Social Exchange Theory (Blau, 1964). Together with Gouldner's (1960) Reciprocity Theory, these conceptualizations help explain employees' behaviors and attitudes toward work vis-à-vis perceived organizational support. When employees realize that their workplace meets their needs, they are likely to develop feelings of obligation and reciprocate with increased devotion and effort. More specifically, when employees feel secure that their physical, emotional, or social needs are taken care of, they feel safe to report transparently on their work processes and results and accept feedback with little worry about potential repercussions. In response to perceived organizational support, employees may also put more emphasis on their professional development, aspiring to perform according to the highest standards for their own success as well as helping the organization to attain its goals. In sum, they would tend to be more accountable. Therefore, we expect in our study that the more teachers and principals perceive organizational support, the higher would be their external as well as internal accountability at work.

It is noteworthy that most of the past studies on relations between organizational support and job attitudes and behaviors in education refer to non-managerial ranks, in particular teachers. However, we may infer effects of principals' perceived organizational support from studies focused on various work factors in principals' work environment. For example, Liu and Bellibas (2018), in their secondary analysis of the Teaching and Learning International Survey (TALIS) 2013 data, found that the availability of work resources such as funding resources and autonomy in staffing varied per country and were related to principals' job satisfaction and organizational commitment. We may speculate that these two work resources represent certain forms of support from higher up the organizational ladder, for example their school boards. In another study, Wang et al. (2018) found that Canadian principals' job satisfaction under work intensification conditions was related to 'maintenance' factors, such as respect from board staff and securing superintendents' approval for new programs and activities – again, factors that may indicate organizational support. Finally, in a study of U.S. principals, Chang et al. (2015) reported that autonomy support by superintendents was positively related to principals' affective organizational commitment, job satisfaction, and intent to stay on the job. Results of these studies indicate that various forms of organizational support in principals' work environment do contribute to productive job attitudes. Thus, we may expect that such support forms would inspire principals' tendency to feel externally and internally accountable.

Organizational support, to sum up, was included in the present study as an additional independent variable. Because of the significant role of organizational support in explaining a wide variety of organizational behaviors and attitudes, it seemed that the introduction of this variable in the study model serves two purposes. First, inclusion of a strong accountability predictor such as organizational support could help clarify and interpret the strength of any significant effect of the key model antecedents – the cultural values. Second, based on findings on moderating effects of organizational support (Wikhamn & Hall, 2014), we could also explore the possibility that organizational support enhances relations between cultural values and accountability dispositions through interaction effects.

3 Study methods

Joris G.J. Beek, Zehava Rosenblatt, Chris Phielix, and Theo Wubbels

Introduction

In the present chapter, we describe the methods that address our research questions listed in the introduction (Chapter 1) in regard to teachers' and principals' accountability. We made sure that these methods best investigate the following topics, so that credible conclusions may be drawn.

1 Accountability as a two-dimensional concept.
2 Differences between accountability dispositions, divided by background characteristics such as gender and seniority.
3 Differences in accountability dispositions toward different audiences, in particular parents and school management.
4 Country differences in teachers' and principals' accountability.
5 Country differences in cultural values and organizational support.
6 Prediction of accountability dispositions by two cultural values: individualism and collectivism.
7 Prediction of accountability dispositions by organizational support.
8 Influence of principals' accountability on respective teachers' accountability.

The topics of this research project are not particularly sensitive or controversial, but we were attentive to all ethical research issues regarding human subjects who were involved in this study. It was of utmost importance to us to ensure that the questionnaire items would not include any sensitive content, that respondents would have the right to refuse participation, and that they could quit the study at any time. The approval of respective Institutional Ethics Review Boards (IRBs) in the researchers' academic institutions in each of the participating countries was secured.

The following sections of this chapter present the process of data collection and describe the study's instruments and measures. The last section of this chapter specifies the study's analytical approach taken to explore the study's research questions.

Data collection

We collected data from teachers and their respective principals using a questionnaire as a research tool. In total, 2,554 teachers from 185 schools and 132 principals from 117 schools completed the questionnaires. Data were collected in each participating school from both principals and teacher faculty members so that teachers were matched with their respective principals using identifying codes. This matching enabled analyses that investigated relations between principals and teachers.

Identical questionnaires were distributed in each country, using applicable translation when necessary. In two countries (*Canada* and *China*), data were collected only from teachers, not principals. Table 3.1 shows the specific provinces or regions in which the data were collected in each country and the number of teachers and principals within each sample. In most cases, the data collected were generally representative of the pertinent country in terms of educational structure and educators' background characteristics (gender, age). However, in some cases it was difficult to collect the desired representative data. For example, in the case of *South Africa*, only privileged schools and schools in the Pretoria area accepted our questionnaires, so the sample was comprised of predominantly (but not entirely)

Table 3.1 Provinces or Regions in the Participating Countries and Number of Teachers and Principals

Country	Provinces	Number of Teachers	Number of Principals
Canada	Nova Scotia, Newfoundland, Ontario, and Alberta Provinces	169	0
China	Guangdong, Guangxi, Shaanxi, and Jilin Provinces	266	0
Hungary	The whole country	338	23
Israel	Northern Israel	418	30
Netherlands	The whole country	178	21
South Africa	Gauteng, Pretoria (Tshwane)	315	17
Spain	Catalonia	470	21
Zimbabwe	Harare	400	20

white teachers and principals who were highly educated and trained, and schools were relatively wealthy.

The questionnaire data were processed first into eight separate data sets (for each of the participating countries) that included respondent identification (ID), school ID, country ID, and background variables. The separate data files were combined into three sets of data. The first consisted of teachers' data, the second included principals' data, and the third consisted of a combination of both teachers' and principals' data. This structure enabled a broad spectrum of analyses, with IDs used as a matching mechanism. When data were missing, these were imputed following the procedure described in Appendix 3.1.[1]

Study measures

Two questionnaires, one for teachers and the other for principals, were used in the present study (Appendix 3.2). Psychometric characteristics of all study variables as well as their number in the questionnaire appear in Appendix 3.3. Both questionnaires included the following scales and measures: external accountability disposition (two versions – general and audience focused), internal accountability disposition, individualism, collectivism, organizational support, and background characteristics.[2]

All multiple-item scales were validated in previous research (see later) and checked for reliability in the first stages of the present study. In an effort to ensure that respondents in the different countries were as close as possible to a shared understanding of the main study concepts, the research team spent considerable time in discussing the meaning of accountability and the other key research variables. The questionnaires were originally prepared in Hebrew and then translated into English and from English into the other four study languages: Chinese, Dutch, Hungarian, and Spanish. Translation was performed in a back-and-forth fashion (cf. Davis et al., 2013) and discussions among researchers were carried out in English.

External and internal accountability

A detailed description of the construction and development of the external and internal accountability scales used in this study can be found in Rosenblatt (2017). The scales were tailored for school context and were slightly modified to be used by both teachers and principals. Its external dimension was modeled to apply to two different audiences: school management and parents.

The 13-item *External Accountability* scale intended to measure the tendency to report to external audiences such as the principal, parents, or school management generally (in the case of teachers) and school boards (in the case of principals). The scale included items reflecting key accountability elements (Frink & Ferris, 1998), such as goal setting, performance report, transparency, performance evaluation, and feedback. Scale reliability (Cronbach's α) was .86 for teachers and .84 for principals. A sample item was: *In your work as a teacher, to what extent do you feel that it is your responsibility to be held accountable when your work in the classroom does not meet expectations?*

A short version (seven items) of external accountability was used to assess external accountability to each of two audiences: parents and school management. These audiences were selected because they seemed to be universally the most legitimate stakeholders in teachers' and principals' work environment. The selection of seven items from the original 13-item measure was based on the items' relevancy to the two audiences. Scale reliability (Cronbach's α) in the present study for accountability toward parents and school management was .86 and .87 for teachers and .87 and .90 for principals, respectively.

The seven-item *Internal Accountability* scale intended to measure teachers' and principals' tendency to report to themselves, based on their professional code and work ethics (Firestone & Shipps, 2005). Scale reliability (Cronbach's α) was .82 for teachers and .83 for principals. A sample item was: *In your work (as a teacher), to what extent do you feel that it is your responsibility to be accountable for your teaching in the best possible way?*

Individualism and collectivism

Individual-level values

Each of the scales for individualism and collectivism included four items. *Individualism* measured the degree to which a person tended to adhere to his or her own personal values and aspirations. *Collectivism* measured the degree to which a person tended to adhere to group values and norms. Both scales were adopted from Triandis and Gelfand (1998) with application of their horizontal dimension (where individuals see themselves as equal to others, in contrast to being placed in a hierarchy). Scale reliability in the present study for individualism and collectivism was α=.74 and α=.81 for teachers and α=.82 and α=.82 for principals, respectively (after deleting item 39 for the principals, see Appendix 3.2). A sample item for individualism was: *I'd rather depend on myself than on others*, and for collectivism was: *The well-being of my fellow (teachers) is important to me.*

Country-level values

As outlined in Chapter 2, we investigated whether country and country-level cultural values may explain teachers' and principals' accountability dispositions. The present study used two country-wide databases. One database was an aggregation of individual teachers and principals in our study, grouped by their respective countries. The other database was borrowed from an external data source.

Country cultural values are often established based on measurement of values with surveys administered to rather large samples (e.g., House et al., 2004; over 17,000 respondents). The two most commonly used sources for country aggregates of cultural values are the databases of the Global Leadership and Organizational Behavior Effectiveness (GLOBE) project (e.g., House et al., 2004, 2014) and the Hofstede studies originating from his work with IBM personnel (e.g., Hofstede et al., 2010). Hofstede and his colleagues keep an updated measure of cultural values on their website, but in their database one country from our sample is missing (*Zimbabwe*) and one is only represented with an estimated value (*Hungary*).[3]

We therefore turned to the GLOBE project for the values that may be most similar to the values we have used in our study. For this purpose, we selected the country scores of the 2004 study and not the more recent scores from 2014 because the latter only refer to chief executive officers (CEOs), whereas the 2004 data are from a broader sample including managers at different organizational levels.

Of the GLOBE's 2004 values, we could only use collectivism defined by House et al. (2004) as the degree to which a person is integrated into groups or families. In a collectivistic society, people would give preference to group interests, and group norms would typically determine their behavior, thoughts, and feelings, whereas in individualistic societies, people are supposed to look after themselves or, alternatively, adhere to personal aspirations, autonomy, freedom, independence, and achievement orientation. Of the nine dimensions of cultural values in the GLOBE project (House et al., 2004), none seems connected to our individualism measure. The *in-group collectivism* scale of the GLOBE project is the most closely connected to the concept of collectivism that we used in our analyses. It describes the degree to which individuals in a certain society express pride, loyalty, and cohesiveness in their organizations or families.[4] The GLOBE project distinguishes between cultural values in practice ('as it is') and desired values ('as it should be'). In this project, it was assumed that leadership was much more connected to the latter (further referred to as values) than to the former because a key mission of leaders is to strategize and plan for the future. In the present study, we looked at the values in practice as our purpose in this study was to describe individuals' and societies' tendencies and inclinations in the present – the time the study took place.

Organizational support

This six-item measure was borrowed from the notion of organizational support, conceived by Eisenberger et al. (1986). Applied to schools, this measure assessed the degree to which teachers perceived school administration (in the case of teachers) and school boards (in the case of principals) as supportive of their work. Reliability in the present study was $\alpha=.88$ for teachers (after deleting items 39 and 42; see Appendix 3.2) and $\alpha=.91$ for principals (after deleting items 32 and 35; see Appendix 3.2). A sample item from the teacher questionnaire was: *My school administration is willing to help me when I need a special favor.*

Background variables

Several background variables were collected in this study for both teachers and principals, and were used as control variables: gender (with females coded 0 and males 1), seniority (work experience in years), and school size (the student body of the school). Data about age were also collected, although the high correlation between age and seniority led to a decision to use the latter for its higher relevancy to our study. We also collected data on schools' religiosity and teachers' school responsibilities (other than teaching). Because *China* did not provide data on school religiosity (only secular schools exist in this country), and there was a high missing-data rate in other countries, we eliminated this variable from our analyses. Finally, teachers' school responsibility (other than teaching) was also eliminated because no data on this variable were collected in *Spain* and *Zimbabwe*.

Analytical approach

In this section, we provide information about the study's multilevel models and describe the statistical procedures used while developing the analytical strategy. First, we discuss the leveled structure of the data and then we specify the full process of the models' design: teachers' external and internal accountability models, principals' external and internal accountability models, and teachers' and principals' models for accountability toward parents and school management. In Chapter 4 – Study Findings, only the final models are presented.

Leveled structure of the teacher data

Given the three-way nesting of the data – teachers within schools within countries – hierarchical linear models (HLM) seemed to be necessary in order to predict teachers' accountability dispositions. However, because of the small number of countries (eight), we could not include the country level in the models (Maas & Hox, 2005). An effort to include countries as dummy variables at the school level also failed because of a collinearity problem (country and other school variables being highly correlated), making the results unreliable. The teachers' data, therefore, were analyzed using two levels: a teacher level, composed of individual teachers' scores, and a teacher faculty level, where school teacher scores were aggregated as school means (Hox et al., 2017), further referred to as school level. To test the applicability of this modeled structure for the teacher analyses, we first calculated the intraclass correlations (ICC) between levels. These analyses, reported in Appendix 3.4, were conducted using HLM 6 (Raudenbush et al., 2004). For all other analyses, we used IBM SPSS Statistics for Windows, Version 25.0.

Predicting teachers' accountability dispositions

Two models were employed to predict teachers' external and internal accountability dispositions by cultural values, organizational support, and background variables. One model included independent variables taken from teachers only. The other included, in addition, independent variables taken from teachers' matched principals and describing the principals' accountability dispositions. In other words, the second model enabled prediction of teacher accountability not only by teachers' cultural values, experienced organizational support, and their background variables, but also by principals' own external and internal accountability. Because, as stated earlier, only six countries provided principal data, the second model included teacher independent variables taken from the principals' country pool, excluding *Canada* and *China*, that had provided only teacher and not principal data.

Looking at the amount of variance in the teacher data for both eight and six countries (Appendix 3.4), it appeared that for all analyses the amount of variance at the school level was significant and, therefore, HLMs had to be applied. Residual plots of all final models for external and internal accountability showed no deviations from normality and linearity.[5]

At the first (teacher) level in the hierarchical linear regression models, we entered gender, seniority, individualism, collectivism, and organizational support as predictors of teachers' external and internal accountability. At the second (school) level, we entered school size, the school means of organizational support, individualism, and collectivism (Centering at the Grand Mean, CGM) to test the influence of these predictors of accountability of individual teachers in their schools. At the first level, the procedure Centering Within Cluster (CWC) was chosen over CGM because the first-level predictors were the main interest of this study (Enders & Tofighi, 2007). When CWC is used, first-level predictors provide information on variables compared to their within group meaning. Thus, regression coefficients are provided that give information about individual teachers compared to their school mean. So, positive coefficients mean that teachers with a higher score for that predictor show a higher accountability score compared to their within school colleagues. Predictors at the second level provide information at the second level (school). A positive coefficient of a second level predictor should be interpreted so that scoring above the sample mean of that predictor results in a higher *school mean score* for accountability.

After testing the models with these predictors, we included the interaction effects of individualism and organizational support and of collectivism and organizational support. Both were included at the first and second level; at the second level, the interaction represented the interaction between variable means. In Appendix 3.5, we present all models that were tested stepwise to get to the final predicting models for both external and internal accountability.

After calculating the models with only teacher and school variables, we calculated models including principals' external and internal accountability scores as school level variables to predict teachers' accountability scores. *Canada* and *China* were left out of this particular analysis, as mentioned earlier. The models were designed in a stepwise fashion to enable comparison with the models in which all teachers were included.

Predicting teachers' accountability dispositions toward parents and school management

Following the statistical models predicting external accountability for teachers, we analyzed in a similar way teachers' accountability, focusing on parents and school management. Similar to the analyses described previously, we first calculated the intercept model which showed the amount of variance located at both the teacher and school level in order to check whether the leveled structure of the data had to be taken into account. As Appendix 3.4 shows, this was indeed the case. Residual plots of all final models for accountability toward parents and school management showed no deviations from normality and linearity.[6] The models for teachers' accountability toward parents and school management are presented in Appendix 3.6.

Predicting principals' accountability dispositions

The principal data base in our study was different than the teacher data base. First, most of the schools that participated in this study (117 in number) included one principal per school (N=107), eight schools included two principals (or co-principals), and two schools included three principals. Second, the principal sample included only six countries (unlike the eight countries in the teacher study). Because of the low numbers of schools with two or more principals and of countries where we could not apply multilevel analyses pertaining to principals, we could not check on the variance distribution over different levels. Accordingly, we employed different analyses to answer the same study questions.

We analyzed the principals' data using traditional linear regression models (Maas & Hox, 2005) to predict principals' external and internal accountability dispositions and accountability toward parents and school management. The variables used as predictors in the teachers' models were also included here (with minor adaptations to principals' milieu, as needed). We used stepwise inclusion to get to the final models. We first entered background variables (gender, seniority, and school size) followed by the scale variables cultural values (individualism and collectivism) and organizational support. For seniority and scale variables, centered values were used in the prediction models. Finally, we entered dummy variables for each country, with *Hungary* as the reference country because the mean country score of *Hungary* was closest to the sample means of both external and internal accountability.

Appendix 3.1
Handling of missing data

The common approach to handling missing data is to delete all cases having missing data. However, in an attempt to adopt statisticians' (e.g., Peeters et al., 2015; Van Buuren, 2018) recommendation to upgrade our work, we tried to employ known methods and software for handling incomplete data problems. As specified in this chapter, our study included three data sets: (1) the teacher data set for eight countries, (2) the principal data set for six countries, and (3) the combined data set of teachers and principals, also for six countries. Within the teacher data, missing items ranged from 4.8% to 0.1%. Of all 2,554 cases, 18.7% had no missing values. Overall, 95.5% of the data was included within the teacher data set. Similar to the teacher data set, all variables in the principal data set had a small percentage of missing data ranging from 7.6% to 0.8%. For principals, 84 cases (63.6%) had no missing values and of all the data (95.8%) was included in the data set.

The combined data set included all principals, but only teachers from schools of which the respective principal(s) completed the questionnaire, amounting to 1,894 teachers (78.4% of all teachers). Missing data in the combined data set ranged from 4.8% to 0.1%. Of all cases, 64.3% had one or more missing values within the questionnaire. Overall, 97.0% of the teacher data was included within the combined data set.

Multiple imputation is broadly recommended as the best general method to deal with incomplete data (Van Buuren, 2018). We used IBM SPSS Statistics for Windows, Version 25.0 (IBM Corp., 2017) to impute the incomplete cases based on all variables included within the regression analyses. With a small amount of missing data, substantive conclusions are unlikely to change with more than five imputations (Van Buuren, 2018) and, therefore, we chose to calculate five imputations for each missing value. Furthermore, we chose to impute the question items over the scale variables to retain as much of the original data as possible. The amounts of missing data we imputed ranged from 4.8% to 0.1%, which we considered a small amount.

Appendix 3.2

The questionnaires used in the study (English version)

Items indicated with an asterisk (*) have been removed in the analyses.

Teacher questionnaire

School code: _____

Part A. Background

a. Gender: 1. Male 2. Female
b. Age: ___ (yrs)
c. Experience as a teacher: ___ (yrs)
d. Tenure (permanent position): yes/no/not relevant
e. If applicable, please specify which leadership position you hold in addition to teaching (e.g., vice-principal, headmaster, subject-area coordinator): _____
f. Teaching area:

   1. _____ Humanities, languages, and social studies
   2. _____ Science, mathematics, and technology
   3. _____ Arts, sport
   4. _____ Other

g. Size of school in number of students: _____
h. School location: 1. Urban 2. Suburban 3. Rural 4. Other _____
i. School level:

   1. _____ Elementary/primary
   2. _____ Middle
   3. _____ High/secondary

j. School religion:

   1. _____ Secular
   2. _____ Religious

Part B. In your work as a teacher, to what extent do you feel that it is your responsibility to:

		Very Little	Little	Neither Little nor Large	Large	Very Large
1	Make sure your students achieve high achievement scores	1	2	3	4	5
2	Meet expected standards	1	2	3	4	5
3	Be accountable for your students' achievements	1	2	3	4	5
4	Report to *school leadership* on the way you perform your work	1	2	3	4	5
5	Report to *other teachers* on the way you perform your work	1	2	3	4	5
6	Report to *parents* on the way you perform your work	1	2	3	4	5
7	Allow your work in class to be transparent to school leadership	1	2	3	4	5
8	Allow your work in class to be transparent to *other teachers*	1	2	3	4	5
9	Allow your work in class to be transparent to *parents*	1	2	3	4	5
10	Be evaluated on the basis of your work achievements	1	2	3	4	5
11	Change your work according to feedback you receive	1	2	3	4	5
12	Be held accountable when your work in the classroom does not meet expectations	1	2	3	4	5
13	Be acknowledged for the success of your classes	1	2	3	4	5

38 Study methods

Part C. In your work as a teacher, to what extent do you feel that it is your duty to:

		Very Little	Little	Neither Little nor Much	Much	Very Much
14	Achieve professional goals	1	2	3	4	5
15	Develop professionally (training sessions, workshops, conferences, etc.)	1	2	3	4	5
16	Learn from the work of outstanding colleagues	1	2	3	4	5
17	Be responsible for teaching in the best possible way	1	2	3	4	5
18	Be responsible for using professional knowledge in your work	1	2	3	4	5
19	Be accountable to your own inner moral standards	1	2	3	4	5
20	Be accountable to professional ethics	1	2	3	4	5

Part D. To what extent do you believe your work should include the following behaviors and activities with regard to school management and parents:

		School Management Very Little / Little / Neither Little nor Much / Much / Very Much	Parents Very Little / Little / Neither Little nor Much / Much / Very Much
21	Strive to achieve set goals	1 2 3 4 5	1 2 3 4 5
22	Report on your performance regarding students' academic achievements	1 2 3 4 5	1 2 3 4 5

	School Management					Parents				
	Very Little	Little	Neither Little nor Much	Much	Very Much	Very Little	Little	Neither Little nor Much	Much	Very Much
23 Report on performance regarding curriculum coverage	1	2	3	4	5	1	2	3	4	5
24 Report on performance regarding social climate (e.g., student behavior, discipline) in class	1	2	3	4	5	1	2	3	4	5
25 Show transparency in your work	1	2	3	4	5	1	2	3	4	5
26 Get formal evaluations on the results of your work	1	2	3	4	5	1	2	3	4	5
27 Get feedback on your teaching	1	2	3	4	5	1	2	3	4	5

Part E. Please indicate how much you agree or disagree with the following statements about your work:

	Strongly Disagree	Disagree	Neither Agree nor Disagree	Agree	Strongly Agree
28 The way I teach in my class is determined for the most part by myself	1	2	3	4	5
29 The contents taught in my class are those that I select myself	1	2	3	4	5
30 My teaching focuses on goals and objectives that I select myself	1	2	3	4	5
31 I myself select the teaching materials that I use with my students	1	2	3	4	5

(*Continued*)

(Continued)

		Strongly Disagree	Disagree	Neither Agree nor Disagree	Agree	Strongly Agree
32	I am free to be creative in my teaching approach	1	2	3	4	5
33	My job does not allow for much discretion on my part	1	2	3	4	5
34	In my class, I have little control over how classroom space is used	1	2	3	4	5
35	My school management strongly supports my goals and values	1	2	3	4	5
36	My school administration values my contribution	1	2	3	4	5
37	My school administration takes pride in my accomplishments at work	1	2	3	4	5
38	My school administration really cares about me	1	2	3	4	5
39	If given the chance, my school administration would take unfair advantage of me	1	2	3	4	5
40	My school administration is willing to help me when I need a special favor	1	2	3	4	5
41	Upon my request, my school administration would change my working conditions, if this is at all possible	1	2	3	4	5
42	My school administration would ignore any complaint from me	1	2	3	4	5

Part F. The following items refer to your personal values and attitudes toward work and life in general. Please indicate how much you agree or disagree with the following statements:

	Strongly Disagree	Disagree	Neither Agree nor Disagree	Agree	Strongly Agree
43 I'd rather depend on myself than on others	1	2	3	4	5
44 I rely on myself more than on others most of the time	1	2	3	4	5
45 I often do 'my own thing'	1	2	3	4	5
46 My personal identity, independent of others, is very important to me	1	2	3	4	5
47 If a fellow teacher gets an award, I would feel proud	1	2	3	4	5
48 The well-being of my fellow teachers is important to me	1	2	3	4	5
49 I take pleasure in spending time with others	1	2	3	4	5
50 I feel good when I cooperate with others	1	2	3	4	5
51 I believe that a person's influence is based primarily on his or her ability and contribution to society and not on the authority of his or her position	1	2	3	4	5
52 I believe that followers are expected to obey their leaders without reservation rather than question their leaders when in disagreement	1	2	3	4	5
53 I believe that people in positions of power try to increase their social distance (hierarchical space) from less powerful individuals	1	2	3	4	5

(*Continued*)

42 *Study methods*

(Continued)

	Strongly Disagree	Disagree	Neither Agree nor Disagree	Agree	Strongly Agree
54 I believe that rank and hierarchical position should go with special privileges	1	2	3	4	5
55 I find orderliness and consistency more important than experimentation or innovation	1	2	3	4	5
56 I tend to lead a highly structured life with few unexpected events	1	2	3	4	5
57 When I have to do something, I prefer to receive instructions that are spelled out in detail, so that I know what I am expected to do	1	2	3	4	5
58 I like to live with laws that cover almost all situations (rather than very few situations)	1	2	3	4	5

Principal questionnaire

School code _____

Part A. Background

a. Gender: 1. Male 2. Female
b. Age: ___ (yrs)
c. Experience as a principal: ___ (yrs)
d. Size of school in number of students: _____
e. School location: 1. Urban 2. Suburban 3. Rural 4. Other ____
f. School level:

   1. _____Elementary/primary
   2. _____Middle
   3. _____High/secondary

g. School religion:

   1. _____Secular
   2. _____Religious

Part B. In your work as a principal, to what extent do you feel that it is your responsibility to:

		Very Little	Little	Neither Little nor Much	Much	Very Much
1	Make sure school academic performance is high	1	2	3	4	5
2	Meet expected standards	1	2	3	4	5
3	Be accountable for the academic achievements of your school students	1	2	3	4	5
4	Report to *superiors* (*superintendent, central education office*) on the way you perform your work	1	2	3	4	5
5	Report to *your teaching staff* on the way you perform your work	1	2	3	4	5
6	Report to *parents* on the way you perform your work	1	2	3	4	5
7	Allow your work in school to be transparent to school leadership	1	2	3	4	5
8	Allow your work in school to be transparent to *other principals*	1	2	3	4	5
9	Allow your work in school to be transparent to *parents*	1	2	3	4	5
10	Be evaluated on the basis of your work achievements	1	2	3	4	5
11	Change your work according to feedback you get	1	2	3	4	5
12	Be held accountable when your work in school does not meet expectations	1	2	3	4	5
13	Be acknowledged for the success of your school	1	2	3	4	5

Part C. In your work as a principal, to what extent do you feel that it is your duty to:

		Very Little	Little	Neither Little nor Much	Much	Very Much
14	Achieve professional goals	1	2	3	4	5
15	Develop professionally (training sessions, workshops, conferences, etc.)	1	2	3	4	5
16	Learn from the work of outstanding colleagues	1	2	3	4	5
17	Be responsible for leading in the best possible way	1	2	3	4	5
18	Be responsible for using professional knowledge in your work	1	2	3	4	5
19	Be accountable to your own personal moral standards	1	2	3	4	5
20	Be accountable to professional ethics	1	2	3	4	5

Part D. To what extent do you believe your work should include the following behaviors and activities with regard to school management board and parents:

		School Management Board — Very Little	Little	Neither Little nor Much	Much	Very Much	Parents — Very Little	Little	Neither Little nor Much	Much	Very Much
21	Strive to achieve set goals	1	2	3	4	5	1	2	3	4	5
22	Report on your performance regarding students' academic achievements	1	2	3	4	5	1	2	3	4	5
23	Report on performance regarding curriculum coverage	1	2	3	4	5	1	2	3	4	5

		School Management Board					Parents				
		Very Little	Little	Neither Little nor Much	Much	Very Much	Very Little	Little	Neither Little nor Much	Much	Very Much
24	Report on performance regarding social climate (e.g., student behavior, discipline) in class	1	2	3	4	5	1	2	3	4	5
25	Show transparency in your work	1	2	3	4	5	1	2	3	4	5
26	Get formal evaluations on the results of your work	1	2	3	4	5	1	2	3	4	5
27	Get feedback on your work as a school principal	1	2	3	4	5	1	2	3	4	5

Part E. Please indicate to what extent you agree or disagree with the following statements about your work:

		Strongly Disagree	Disagree	Neither Agree nor Disagree	Agree	Strongly Agree
28	My school board strongly supports my goals and values	1	2	3	4	5
29	My school board values my contribution	1	2	3	4	5
30	My school board takes pride in my accomplishments at work	1	2	3	4	5
31	My school board really cares about me	1	2	3	4	5
32	If given the chance, my school board would take unfair advantage of me	1	2	3	4	5

(*Continued*)

(Continued)

		Strongly Disagree	Disagree	Neither Agree nor Disagree	Agree	Strongly Agree
33	My school board is willing to help me when I need a special favor	1	2	3	4	5
34	If I asked, my school board would change my working conditions, if this is at all possible	1	2	3	4	5
35	My school board would ignore any complaint from me	1	2	3	4	5

Part F. The following items refer to your personal values and attitudes toward work and life in general. Please indicate how much you agree or disagree with the following statements:

		Strongly Disagree	Disagree	Neither Agree nor Disagree	Agree	Strongly Agree
36	I'd rather depend on myself than others	1	2	3	4	5
37	I rely on myself more than others most of the time	1	2	3	4	5
38	I often do 'my own thing'	1	2	3	4	5
39	My personal identity, independent of others, is very important to me*	1	2	3	4	5
40	If a colleague principal gets an award, I would feel proud	1	2	3	4	5
41	The well-being of my colleague principals is important to me	1	2	3	4	5
42	I take pleasure in spending time with others	1	2	3	4	5

		Strongly Disagree	Disagree	Neither Agree nor Disagree	Agree	Strongly Agree
43	I feel good when I cooperate with others	1	2	3	4	5
44	I believe that a person's influence is based primarily on one's ability and contribution to society and not on the authority of one's position	1	2	3	4	5
45	I believe that followers are expected to obey their leaders without reservation rather than question their leaders when in disagreement	1	2	3	4	5
46	I believe that people in positions of power try to increase their social distance (hierarchical space) from less powerful individuals	1	2	3	4	5
47	I believe that rank and hierarchical position should go with special privileges	1	2	3	4	5
48	I find orderliness and consistency more important than experimentation or innovation	1	2	3	4	5
49	I tend to lead a highly structured life with few unexpected events	1	2	3	4	5
50	When I have to do something, I prefer to receive instructions that are spelled out in detail, so I know what I am expected to do	1	2	3	4	5
51	I like to live with laws that cover almost all situations (rather than very few situations)	1	2	3	4	5

48 Study methods

Part G. Please indicate the degree to which you perceive autonomy in your work:

		\multicolumn{5}{c}{Perceived Autonomy}				
		Very Little	Little	Neither Little nor Much	Much	Very Much
52	Determining number/type of faculty and staff	1	2	3	4	5
53	Allocating resources	1	2	3	4	5
54	Hiring faculty and staff	1	2	3	4	5
55	Assigning faculty and staff	1	2	3	4	5
56	Transferring and/or discharging unsuitable faculty and staff	1	2	3	4	5
57	Allocating time for instruction	1	2	3	4	5
58	Determining student discipline policies/ procedures	1	2	3	4	5

Appendix 3.3
Psychometric and questionnaire position of study variables

Study methods

Scale	Sub-dimensions	Teacher Questionnaire (item numbers)	Principal Questionnaire (item numbers)	Teachers Original	Teachers After Imputation	Principals Original	Principals After Imputation
External accountability	Setting goals/meeting standards	1–3	1–3	.698	.699	.810	.804
	Report on performance	4–6	4–6	.726	.724	.711	.713
	Transparency	7–9	7–9	.810	.810	.702	.694
	Evaluation and feedback	10–13	10–13	.717	.717	.613	.604
	Combined			.861	.858	.839	.837
Internal accountability	Professional code	14–18	14–18	.800	.800	.771	.774
	Work ethic	19–20	19–20	.735	.735	.806	.809
	Combined			.822	.821	.832	.833
External accountability toward	Managers	21–27	21–27	.872	.870	.899	.896
	Parents			.865	.864	.871	.868
Organizational support		35–42	28–35	.882	.883	.910	.909
Individualism		44–46	36–39	.741	.739	.822	.816
Collectivism		47–50	40–43	.808	.809	.825	.823

Appendix 3.4
Check on leveled structure teacher data

In order to check if multilevel analyses were needed, the variance distributions for the teacher data on the teacher and school level were tested by calculating the intraclass correlation (ICC) between levels. The results in the following table showed that the variance at the school level was substantial in all data sets and, thus, multilevel analyses were needed.

	Variance Component Teacher (First) Level, σ_e^2	School (Second) Level, $\sigma_{u_0}^2$	Proportion of Variance[1] Teacher Level	School Level	Intraclass Correlation (ICC)
8 countries					
External accountability	0.26688	0.06381	80.7	19.3	0.19 $\chi^2(184): 783.85$
Internal accountability	0.19220	0.04932	79.6	20.4	0.20 $\chi^2(184): 794.70$
Accountability toward parents	0.55292	0.07874	87.7	12.3	0.12 $\chi^2(184): 523.24$
Accountability toward school management	0.34598	0.11410	75.2	24.8	0.25 $\chi^2(184): 951.25$
6 countries					
External accountability	0.26745	0.05380	83.3	16.7	0.17 $\chi^2(116): 498.59$
Internal accountability	0.18732	0.03934	82.6	17.4	0.17 $\chi^2(116): 513.07$
Accountability toward parents	0.56452	0.08301	87.1	12.8	0.13 $\chi^2(116): 386.37$
Accountability toward school management	0.35044	0.10983	76.1	23.9	0.24 $\chi^2(116): 676.21$

$$Variance_{Teacher} = \frac{\sigma_e^2}{\sigma_e^2 + \sigma_{u_0}^2} \qquad Variance_{School} = \frac{\sigma_{u_0}^2}{\sigma_e^2 + \sigma_{u_0}^2}$$

Note: [1] Variance at all level-2 ($\sigma_{u_0}^2$) were significant at the 0.01 level.

Appendix 3.5a
Models for teachers' external accountability

1. Without Principals' Accountability, Eight Countries

Fixed Part	M1 Intercept B(SE)	M2 M1 + Background B(SE)	M2 p	M3 M2 + Cult. Values and Org. Support B(SE)	M3 p	M4 M3 + Teacher Level Interactions B(SE)	M4 p	M5 M4 + School Size B(SE)	M5 p	M6 M5 + School Cult. Values and Org. Support B(SE)	M6 p	M7 M6 + School Level Interactions B(SE)	M7 p	M7 β
Intercept	3.9 (0.022)	3.92 (0.024)		3.91 (0.024)		3.91 (0.024)		3.9 (0.024)		3.9 (0.022)		3.91 (0.022)		
Gender		−0.05 (0.024)	.056	−0.03 (0.023)	.129	−0.03 (0.023)	.132	−0.03 (0.023)	.133	−0.03 (0.023)	.2	−0.03 (0.023)	.174	−0.01
Seniority		0.003 (0.001)	.029	0.002 (0.001)	.037	0.003 (0.001)	.032	0.002 (0.001)	.049	0.002 (0.001)	.088	0.002 (0.001)	.09	0.02
Individualism				−0.003 (0.015)	.861	−0.0008 (0.014)	.954	−0.0006 (0.014)	.966	−0.0002 (0.014)	.989	−0.0003 (0.014)	.981	−0.0003
Collectivism				0.2 (0.021)	<.001	0.21 (0.021)	<.001	0.21 (0.021)	<.001	0.21 (0.021)	<.001	0.21 (0.021)	<.001	0.12
Organizational Support				0.2 (0.018)	<.001	0.2 (0.018)	<.001	0.2 (0.018)	<.001	0.2 (0.018)	<.001	0.2 (0.018)	<.001	0.16
Org. Support x Individualism						0.004 (0.018)	.834	0.004 (0.018)	.833	0.003 (0.018)	.883	0.01 (0.018)	.695	0.03
Org. Support x Collectivism						0.04 (0.025)	.152	0.04 (0.024)	.108	0.04 (0.025)	.088	0.04 (0.025)	.077	0.005
School Size[a]								−0.07 (0.029)	.017	0.03 (0.033)	.433	0.04 (0.034)	.297	0.03
School Mean Individualism										0.1 (0.065)	.118	0.1 (0.058)	.103	0.03
School Mean Collectivism										0.12 (0.087)	.180	0.103 (0.084)	.221	0.027
School Mean Org. Support										0.26 (0.071)	.001	0.27 (0.064)	<.001	0.12

School Mean Individualism x School Mean Org. Support	−0.17 (0.136)	.204	−0.03
School Mean Collectivism x School Mean Org. Support	−0.03 (0.11)	.8	−0.01

Random Part	Variance	Variance	Explained variance	Variance	Explained variance	Variance	Explained variance	Variance	Explained variance	Variance	Explained variance	Variance	Explained variance	Variance	Explained variance
σ_e^2	0.267	0.266	0.4%	0.229	14%	0.228	14%	0.228	14%	0.228	14%	0.228	14%	0.228	14%
$\sigma_{u_0}^2$	0.064	0.064	0	0.067	0	0.068	0	0.065	0	0.046	28%	0.045	30%		

Note: [a] School size was divided by 1,000.

2. With Principals' Accountability, Six Countries

Fixed Part	M1 Intercept B(SE)	M2 M1 + Background B(SE)	M2 p	M3 M2 + Cult Values and Org. Support B(SE)	M3 p	M4 M3 + Teacher Level Interactions B(SE)	M4 p	M5 M4 + School Size B(SE)	M5 p	M6 M5 + School Cult. Values and Org. Support B(SE)	M6 p	M7 M6 + School Level Interactions B(SE)	M7 p	M8 M7 + Principals' Accountability B(SE)	M8 p	β
Intercept	3.94 (0.025)	3.96 (0.027)		3.96 (0.027)		3.95 (0.028)		3.95 (0.028)		3.95 (0.025)		3.93 (0.026)		3.94 (0.024)		
Gender		-0.05 (0.028)	.096	-0.04 (0.027)	.186	-0.04 (0.027)	.182	-0.04 (0.027)	.170	-0.03 (0.027)	.235	-0.03 (0.027)	.257	-0.03 (0.027)	.245	-0.01
Seniority		0.003 (0.002)	.065	0.002 (0.001)	.145	0.002 (0.001)	.129	0.002 (0.001)	.123	0.002 (0.001)	.190	0.002 (0.001)	.221	0.002 (0.001)	.181	0.02
Individualism				0.008 (0.016)	.621	0.01 (0.016)	.489	0.01 (0.016)	.489	0.01 (0.016)	.479	0.01 (0.016)	.486	0.01 (0.016)	.491	0.01
Collectivism				0.19 (0.024)	<.001	0.20 (0.025)	<.001	0.20 (0.025)	<.001	0.20 (0.024)	<.001	0.20 (0.024)	<.001	0.20 (0.024)	<.001	0.11
Org. Support				0.20 (0.021)	<.001	0.20 (0.021)	<.001	0.20 (0.021)	<.001	0.20 (0.021)	<.001	0.20 (0.021)	<.001	0.20 (0.021)	<.001	0.15
Org. Support x Individualism						0.01 (0.019)	.685	0.01 (0.019)	.687	0.01 (0.020)	.688	0.005 (0.020)	.807	0.003 (0.020)	.823	0.003
Org. Support x Collectivism						0.06 (0.031)	.057	0.06 (0.031)	.054	0.06 (0.033)	.061	0.06 (0.033)	.085	0.06 (0.033)	.091	0.03
School Size[a]								0.06 (0.053)	.226	0.11 (0.047)	.022	0.11 (0.05)	.023	0.09 (0.049)	.075	0.04
School Mean Individualism										0.04 (0.062)	.494	0.03 (0.064)	.602	0.04 (0.058)	.440	0.01
School Mean Collectivism										0.06 (0.093)	.551	0.056 (0.093)	.550	0.025 (0.085)	.772	0.005
School Mean Org. Support										0.35 (0.07)	<.001	0.34 (0.07)	<.001	0.30 (0.064)	<.001	0.11

	Variance	Variance	Expl. variance	Variance	Expl. variance	Variance	Expl. variance	Variance	Expl. variance	Variance	Expl. variance	Variance	Expl. variance	Variance	Expl. variance
School Mean Individualism x School Mean Org. Support										0.12 (0.163)	.461	0.09 (0.145)	.541		0.01
School Mean Collectivism x School Mean Org. Support										0.48 (0.236)	.045	0.33 (0.226)	.144		0.03
Principal External Accountability												0.16 (0.051)	.002		0.07
Random Part	Variance	Variance	Expl. variance	Variance	Expl. variance	Variance	Expl. variance	Variance	Expl. variance	Variance	Expl. variance	Variance	Expl. variance	Variance	Expl. variance
σ_e^2	0.267	0.266	0.4%	0.229	15%	0.228	15%	0.228	15%	0.228	15%	0.228	15%	0.228	15%
$\sigma_{u_0}^2$	0.054	0.054	0	0	0	0.056	0	0.054	0	0.037	0	0.035	31%	0.031	43%

Note: [a] School size was divided by 1,000.

Appendix 3.5b
Models for teachers' internal accountability

1. Without Principals' Accountability, Eight Countries

	M1	M2		M3		M4		M5		M6		M7		
	Intercept	M1 + Background		M2 + Cult. Values and Org. Support		M3 + Teacher Level Interactions		M4 + School Size		M5 + School Cult. Values and Org. Support		M6 + School Level Interactions		
Fixed Part	B(SE)	p	B(SE)	p	B(SE)	p	B(SE)	p	B(SE)	p	B(SE)	p	B(SE)	p	β
Intercept	4.46 (0.019)	0	4.48 (0.02)	0	4.48 (0.02)	0	4.48 (0.02)	0	4.48 (0.02)	0	4.48 (0.016)	0	4.49 (0.017)	0	
Gender			−0.06 (0.02)	.003	−0.04 (0.018)	.019	−0.04 (0.018)	.019	−0.04 (0.018)	.016	−0.04 (0.018)	.025	−0.04 (0.018)	.018	−0.02
Seniority			0.002 (0.001)	.036	0.002 (0.001)	.059	0.002 (0.001)	.066	0.001 (0.001)	.127	0.001 (0.001)	.194	0.001 (0.001)	.180	0.01
Individualism					0.029 (0.014)	.036	0.03 (0.014)	.050	0.03 (0.014)	.048	0.03 (0.014)	.045	0.03 (0.014)	.042	0.02
Collectivism					0.23 (0.019)	<.001	0.23 (0.018)	<.001	0.23 (0.018)	<.001	0.23 (0.018)	<.001	0.23 (0.018)	<.001	0.13
Organizational Support					0.08 (0.014)	<.001	0.08 (0.014)	<.001	0.08 (0.014)	<.001	0.08 (0.014)	<.001	0.08 (0.014)	<.001	0.07
Org. Support x Individualism							−0.001 (0.017)	.975	−0.0003 (0.016)	.987	0.001 (0.017)	.946	0[b] (0.017)	1.00	0[c]
Org. Support x Collectivism							−0.02 (0.023)	.289	−0.02 (0.021)	.33	−0.01 (0.022)	.545	−0.01 (0.022)	.722	0
School Size[a]									−0.1 (0.032)	.002	−0.01 (0.026)	.761	0 (0.025)	.921	0
School Mean Individualism											0.15 (0.046)	.002	0.15 (0.045)	.001	0.05

(Continued)

(Continued)

Fixed Part	M1 Intercept B(SE) p	M2 M1 + Background B(SE) p	Expl. variance	M3 M2 + Cult. Values and Org. Support B(SE) p	Expl. variance	M4 M3 + Teacher Level Interactions B(SE) p	Expl. variance	M5 M4 + School Size B(SE) p	Expl. variance	M6 M5 + School Cult. Values and Org. Support B(SE) p	Expl. variance	M7 M6 + School Level Interactions B(SE) p	β
School Mean Collectivism										0.29 (0.076) <.001		0.27 (0.077) .001	0.07
School mean Organizational Support										0.16 (0.04) <.001		0.16 (0.042) <.001	0.07
School mean Individualism x School Mean Org. Support												0.05 (0.081) .561	0.008
School mean Collectivism x School Mean Org. Support												−0.13 (0.073) .070	−0.03

Random Part	Variance	Variance	Expl. variance	Variance	Expl. variance	Variance	Expl. variance	Variance	Expl. variance	Variance	Expl. variance	Variance	Expl. variance
σ_e^2	0.192	0.192	0%	0.168	13%	0.168	13%	0.168	13%	0.167	13%	0.167	13%
$\sigma_{u_0}^2$	0.049	0.047	0	0.050	0	0.049	0	0.043	12%	0.024	49%	0.023	53%

Note: [a] School size was divided by 1,000, [b] −0.000003, [c] −0.000002.

2. With Principals' Accountability, Six Countries

Fixed Part	M1 Intercept B(SE))	p	M2 M1 + Background B(SE)	p	M3 M2 + Cult. Values and Org. Support B(SE)	p	M4 M3 + Teacher Level Interactions B(SE)	p	M5 M4 + School Size B(SE)	P	M6 M5 + School Cult. Values and Org. Support B(SE)	p	M7 M6 + School Level Interactions B(SE)	p	M8 M7 + Principals' Accountability B(SE)	p	β
Intercept	4.49 (0.021)		4.51 (0.022)		4.51 (0.022)		4.51 (0.022)		4.51 (0.022)		4.51 (0.019)		4.5 (0.021)		4.51 (0.019)		
Gender			−0.07 (0.025)	.007	−0.05 (0.023)	.037	−0.05 (0.023)	.039	−0.05 (0.022)	.040	−0.04 (0.022)	.068	−0.04 (0.022)	.071	−0.04 (0.022)	.066	−0.02
Seniority			0.002 (0.001)	.095	0.001 (0.001)	.210	0.001 (0.001)	.236	0.001 (0.001)	.246	0.001 (0.001)	.340	0.001 (0.001)	.351	0.001 (0.001)	.206	0.01
Individualism					0.037 (0.015)	.017	0.04 (0.016)	.024	0.04 (0.016)	.024	0.04 (0.016)	.022	0.04 (0.016)	.022	0.04 (0.016)	.022	0.03
Collectivism					0.23 (0.022)	<.001	0.22 (0.021)	<.001	0.22 (0.021)	<.001	0.22 (0.021)	<.001	0.22 (0.021)	<.001	0.22 (0.021)	<.001	0.12
Organizational Support					0.08 (0.015)	<.001	0.08 (0.015)	<.001	0.08 (0.015)	<.001	0.08 (0.015)	<.001	0.08 (0.015)	<.001	0.08 (0.015)	<.001	0.06
Org. Support x Individualism							−0.005 (0.02)	.817	−0.005 (0.02)	.820	−0.004 (0.021)	.857	−0.005 (0.021)	.841	−0.005 (0.021)	.818	−0.003
Org. Support x Collectivism							−0.04 (0.032)	.260	−0.04 (0.032)	.256	−0.03 (0.035)	.383	−0.03 (0.035)	.351	−0.03 (0.035)	.367	−0.02
School Size									−0.02 (0.052)	.672	0.03 (0.043)	.488	0.03 (0.044)	.477	0.02 (0.038)	.660	0.004
School Mean Individualism											0.17 (0.054)	.002	0.17 (0.054)	.002	0.16 (0.051)	.002	0.06
School Mean Collectivism											0.31 (0.089)	.001	0.31 (0.088)	.001	0.26 (0.078)	.001	0.06
School Mean Organizational Support											0.15 (0.053)	.006	0.15 (0.055)	.009	0.13 (0.052)	.014	0.04

(Continued)

(Continued)

	M1 Intercept			M2 M1 + Background			M3 M2 + Cult. Values and Org. Support			M4 M3 + Teacher Level Interactions			M5 M4 + School Size			M6 M5 + School Cult. Values and Org. Support			M7 M6 + School Level Interactions			M8 M7 + Principals' Accountability		
Fixed Part	B(SE))	p		B(SE)	p	Expl. variance	B(SE)	p	Expl. variance	B(SE)	p	Expl. variance	B(SE)	p	Expl. variance	B(SE)	p	Expl. variance	B(SE)	p	Expl. variance	B(SE)	p	β
School Mean Individualism x School Mean Org. Support																			-0.004 (0.118)	.972	14%	-0.02 (0.118)	.892	-0.004
School Mean Collectivism x School Mean Org. Support																			0.12 (0.171)	.477	38%	-0.06 (0.167)	.740	-0.001
Principal Internal Accountability																						0.22 (0.044)	<.001	0.07
Random Part	Variance		Expl. variance	Variance		Expl. variance	Variance		Expl. variance	Variance		Expl. variance	Variance		Expl. variance	Variance		Expl. variance	Variance		Expl. variance	Variance		Expl. variance
σ_e^2	0.187			0.187		0%	0.165		12%	0.164		14%	0.164		14%	0.164		14%	0.164		14%	0.164		14%
$\sigma_{u_0}^2$	0.039			0.037		0	0.039		0	0.039		0	0.039		0	0.024		38%	0.024		38%	0.016		58%

Note: [a] School size was divided by 1,000.

Appendix 3.6a
Models for teachers' accountability toward parents

1. Without Principals' Accountability, Eight Countries

Fixed Part	M1 Intercept B(SE)	M1 p	M2 M1 + Background B(SE)	M2 p	M3 M2 + Cult. Values and Org. Support B(SE)	M3 p	M4 M3 + Teacher Level Interactions B(SE)	M4 p	M5 M4 + School Size B(SE)	M5 p	M6 M5 + School Cult. Values and Org. Support B(SE)	M6 p	M7 M6 + School Level Interactions B(SE)	M7 p	β
Intercept	3.67 (0.027)		3.68 (0.028)		3.67 (0.028)		3.67 (0.029)		3.67 (0.029)		3.66 (0.028)		3.66 (0.028)		
Gender			−0.01 (0.035)	.679	0.003 (0.034)	.935	0.003 (0.034)	.921	0.003 (0.034)	.928	0.01 (0.034)	.839	0.01 (0.034)	.834	0.003
Seniority			0.004 (0.002)	.015	0.004 (0.002)	.018	0.004 (0.002)	.018	0.003 (0.002)	.027	0.003 (0.002)	.043	0.003 (0.002)	.045	0.03
Individualism					−0.001 (0.025)	.971	0.001 (0.025)	.958	0.001 (0.025)	.948	0.003 (0.025)	.921	0.002 (0.025)	.933	0.002
Collectivism					0.28 (0.033)	<.001	0.28 (0.034)	<.001	0.28 (0.034)	<.001	0.28 (0.034)	<.001	0.28 (0.034)	<.001	0.16
Organizational Support					0.12 (0.026)	<.001	0.12 (0.026)	<.001	0.12 (0.026)	<.001	0.12 (0.026)	<.001	0.12 (0.026)	<.001	0.09
Org. Support x Individualism							−0.03 (0.026)	.292	−0.03 (0.026)	.295	−0.03 (0.027)	.337	−0.02 (0.027)	.418	−0.01
Org. Support x Collectivism							0.02 (0.031)	.599	0.02 (0.03)	.504	0.04 (0.031)	.258	0.03 (0.032)	.322	0.02
School Size[a]									−0.04 (0.023)	.068	−0.001 (0.022)	.960	−0.003 (0.023)	.889	−0.002
School Mean Individualism											−0.14 (0.079)	.071	−0.15 (0.078)	.059	−0.05
School Mean Collectivism											0.61 (0.098)	<.001	0.61 (0.098)	<.001	0.16
School Mean Organizational Support											−0.06 (0.082)	.441	−0.05 (0.077)	.497	−0.02

	Variance	Expl. variance	Variance	Expl. variance	Variance	Expl. variance	Variance	Expl. variance	Variance	Expl. variance		
School Mean Individualism x School Mean Org. Support											−0.12 (0.184)	.512 −0.02
School Mean Collectivism x School Mean Org. Support											0.09 (0.131)	.498 0.02

Random Part	Variance	Expl. variance	Variance	Expl. variance	Variance	Expl. variance	Variance	Expl. variance	Variance	Expl. variance	Variance	Expl. variance
σ_e^2	0.559		0.557	0.3%	0.523	6%	0.522	7%	0.522	7%	0.521	7%
$\sigma_{u_0}^2$	0.079 <.001		0.079	0	0.083	0	0.083	0	0.081	0	0.061	23%

Note: [a] School size was divided by 1,000.

2. With Principals' Accountability, Six Countries

Fixed Part	M1 Intercept B(SE)	M2 M1 + Background B(SE)	M2 p	M3 M2 + Cult. Values and Org. Support B(SE)	M3 p	M4 M3 + Teacher Level Interactions B(SE)	M4 p	M5 M4 + School Size B(SE)	M5 p	M6 M5 + School Cult. Values and Org. Support B(SE)	M6 p	M7 M6 + School Level Interactions B(SE)	M7 p	M8 M7 + Principals' Accountability B(SE)	M8 p	β
Intercept	3.66 (0.032)	3.66 (0.034)		3.66 (0.034)		3.66 (0.035)		3.66 (0.034)		3.65 (0.033)		3.63 (0.033)		3.63 (0.032)		
Gender		−0.01 (0.043)	.873	0.01 (0.041)	.786	0.01 (0.041)	.784	0.01 (0.041)	.734	0.01 (0.041)	.730	0.01 (0.041)	.760	0.01 (0.041)	.745	0.01
Seniority		0.004 (0.002)	.031	0.003 (0.002)	.058	0.003 (0.002)	.058	0.003 (0.002)	.068	0.003 (0.002)	.085	0.003 (0.002)	.062	0.003 (0.002)	.058	0.03
Individualism				0.006 (0.029)	.838	0.01 (0.029)	.837	0.01 (0.029)	.838	0.01 (0.028)	.823	0.01 (0.029)	.822	0.01 (0.029)	.823	0.005
Collectivism				0.26 (0.037)	<.001	0.25 (0.037)	<.001	0.25 (0.037)	<.001	0.26 (0.037)	<.001	0.26 (0.037)	<.001	0.26 (0.037)	<.001	0.14
Organizational Support				0.11 (0.029)	<.001	0.12 (0.029)	<.001	0.12 (0.029)	<.001	0.12 (0.029)	<.001	0.12 (0.029)	<.001	0.12 (0.029)	<.001	0.09
Org. Support x Individualism						−0.02 (0.033)	.621	−0.02 (0.033)	.633	−0.01 (0.033)	.696	−0.02 (0.033)	.500	−0.02 (0.033)	.521	−0.01
Org. Support x Collectivism						−0.004 (0.041)	.930	−0.01 (0.040)	.896	0.005 (0.042)	.908	0.01 (0.042)	.896	0.005 (0.042)	.914	0.003
School Size[a]								−0.12 (0.074)	.114	−0.08 (0.065)	.207	−0.10 (0.063)	.122	−0.09 (0.063)	.172	−0.04
School Mean Individualism										−0.22 (0.100)	.028	−0.24 (0.092)	.010	−0.22 (0.091)	.019	−0.07
School Mean Collectivism										0.51 (0.118)	<.001	0.49 (0.118)	<.001	0.45 (0.109)	<.001	0.10

	Variance	(SE)	p				
School Mean Organizational Support	0.02	(0.107)	.855	0.01 (0.100) .941	−0.01 (0.095) .915	−0.004	
School Mean Individualism × School Mean Org. Support				0.58 (0.279) .039	0.58 (0.273) .036	0.07	
School Mean Collectivism × School Mean Org. Support				−0.04 (0.393) .924	−0.01 (0.395) .988	−0.001	
Principal External Accountability Toward Parents					0.11 (0.035) .004	0.08	

Random Part	Variance	Expl. variance	Variance	Expl. Variance	Variance	Expl. variance	Variance	Expl. variance	Variance	Expl. variance	Variance	Expl. variance	Variance	Expl. variance	Variance	Expl. variance
σ_e^2	0.565		0.563	0.4%	0.532	6%	0.531	6%	0.531	6%	0.531	6%	0.531	6%	0.531	6%
$\sigma_{u_0}^2$	0.083		0.084	0	0.087	0	0.087	0	0.084	0	0.066	20%	0.061	27%	0.056	33%

Note: [a] School size was divided by 1,000.

Appendix 3.6b
Models for teachers' accountability toward school management

1. Without Principals' Accountability, Eight Countries

Fixed Part	M1 Intercept B(SE)	p	M2 M1 + Background B(SE)	p	M3 M2 + Cult. Values and Org. Support B(SE)	p	M4 M3 + Teacher Level Interactions B(SE)	p	M5 M4 + School Size B(SE)	p	M6 M5 + School Cult. Values and Org. Support B(SE)	p	M7 M6 + School Level Interactions B(SE)	p	β
Intercept	4.07 (0.028)		4.07 (0.031)		4.07 (0.031)		4.07 (0.031)		4.07 (0.031)		4.06 (0.028)		4.07 (0.03)		
Gender			−0.01 (0.023)	.355	0.01 (0.023)	.707	−0.01 (0.023)	.705	−0.01 (0.023)	.679	−0.003 (0.023)	.892	−0.003 (0.023)	.891	−0.001
Seniority			0.002 (0.001)	.075	0.002 (0.001)	.082	0.002 (0.001)	.074	0.002 (0.001)	.135	0.001 (0.001)	.254	0.001 (0.001)	.252	0.01
Individualism					0.008 (0.018)	.630	−0.01 (0.018)	.678	−0.01 (0.018)	.690	−0.01 (0.018)	.711	−0.01 (0.018)	.720	−0.005
Collectivism					0.24 (0.024)	<.001	0.24 (0.023)	<.001	0.24 (0.023)	<.001	0.25 (0.023)	<.001	0.25 (0.023)	<.001	0.14
Organizational Support					0.17 (0.022)	<.001	0.17 (0.022)	<.001	0.17 (0.022)	<.001	0.17 (0.022)	<.001	0.17 (0.022)	<.001	0.13
Org. Support x Individualism							0.005 (0.024)	.830	0.006 (0.023)	.806	0.006 (0.024)	.787	0.004 (0.024)	.868	0.02
Org. Support x Collectivism							0.02 (0.027)	.379	0.03 (0.026)	.288	0.03 (0.027)	.211	0.04 (0.028)	.194	0.003
School Size[a]									−0.09 (0.023)	<.001	0.001 (0.02)	.934	−0.001 (0.022)	.980	−0.0004
School Mean Individualism											0.11 (0.075)	.148	0.11 (0.074)	.124	0.04
School Mean Collectivism											0.30 (0.126)	.018	0.30 (0.13)	.024	0.08

(*Continued*)

(Continued)

Fixed Part	M1 Intercept		M2 M1 + Background		M3 M2 + Cult. Values and Org. Support		M4 M3 + Teacher Level Interactions		M5 M4 + School Size		M6 M5 + School Cult. Values and Org. Support		M7 M6 + School Level Interactions		
	B(SE)	p	B(SE)	p	B(SE)	p	B(SE)	p	B(SE)	p	B(SE)	p	B(SE)	p	β
School Mean Organizational Support											0.25 (0.079)	.002	0.24 (0.079)	.003	0.11
School Mean Individualism x School Mean Org. Support													0.12 (0.143)	.397	0.02
School Mean Collectivism x School Mean Org. Support													-0.07 (0.105)	.504	-0.01

Random Part	Variance	Variance	Variance	Expl. variance	Variance	Expl. variance	Variance	Expl. variance	Variance	Expl. variance	Variance	Expl. variance	Variance	Expl. variance
σ_e^2	0.346	0.345	0.308	0.3%	0.308	10%	0.308	10%	0.308	10%	0.307	11%	0.307	11%
$\sigma_{u_0}^2$	0.114	0.116	0.120	0	0.120	0	0.120	0	0.110	4%	0.084	26%	0.082	28%

Note: [a] School size was divided by 1,000.

2. With Principals' Accountability, Six Countries

Fixed Part	M1 Intercept B(SE) p	M2 M1 + Background B(SE) p	M3 M2 + Cult. Values and Org. Support B(SE) p	M4 M3 + Teacher Level Interactions B(SE) P	M5 M4 + School Size B(SE) p	M6 M5 + School Cult. Values and Org. Support B(SE) p	M7 M6 + School Level Interactions B(SE) p	M8 M7 + Principals' Accountability B(SE) p β
Intercept	4.1 (0.034)	4.11 (0.037)	4.10 (0.037)	4.10 (0.038)	4.10 (0.038)	4.09 (0.036)	4.08 (0.037)	4.08 (0.035)
Gender		-0.02 (0.031) .536	-0.003 (0.029) .909	-0.004 (0.029) .900	-0.004 (0.029) .892	0.002 (0.029) .935	0.002 (0.029) .941	0.003 (0.029) .931 0.001
Seniority		0.002 (0.001) .107	0.002 (0.001) .189	0.002 (0.001) .176	0.002 (0.001) .175	0.001 (0.001) .288	0.001 (0.001) .269	0.001 (0.001) .274 0.01
Individualism			-0.008 (0.02) .700	-0.01 (0.02) .764	-0.01 (0.020) .765	-0.01 (0.020) .778	-0.01 (0.02) .777	-0.01 (0.020) .775 -0.004
Collectivism			0.23 (0.026) <.001	0.24 (0.025) <.001	0.24 (0.025) <.001	0.24 (0.025) <.001	0.24 (0.025) <.001	0.24 (0.025) <.001 0.14
Organizational Support			0.15 (0.025) <.001	0.15 (0.025) <.001	0.15 (0.025) <.001	0.15 (0.025) <.001	0.15 (0.025) <.001	0.15 (0.025) <.001 0.11
Org. Support x Individualism				-0.003 (0.027) .911	-0.003 (0.027) .910	-0.002 (0.028) .944	-0.006 (0.027) .831	-0.005 (0.027) .842 -0.004
Org. Support x Collectivism				0.03 (0.036) .352	0.03 (0.036) .349	0.04 (0.037) .327	0.04 (0.037) .330	0.03 (0.037) .347 0.02
School Size					0.02 (0.089) .811	0.08 (0.081) .325	0.07 (0.083) .394	0.1 (0.083) .247 0.05
School Mean Individualism						0.16 (0.091) .076	0.14 (0.087) .102	0.14 (0.09) .129 0.04
School Mean Collectivism						0.32 (0.170) .061	0.30 (0.160) .060	0.23 (0.153) .136 0.05
School Mean Organizational Support						0.21 (0.107) .057	0.19 (0.111) .091	0.18 (0.104) .077 0.07

(Continued)

(Continued)

Fixed Part	M1 Intercept B(SE) p	M2 M1 + Background B(SE) p	Expl. variance	M3 M2 + Cult. Values and Org. Support B(SE) p	Variance	Expl. variance	M4 M3 + Teacher Level Interactions B(SE) P	Variance	Expl. variance	M5 M4 + School Size B(SE) p	Variance	Expl. variance	M6 M5 + School Cult. Values and Org. Support B(SE) p	Variance	Expl. variance	M7 M6 + School Level Interactions B(SE) p	Variance	Expl. variance	M8 M7 + Principals' Accountability B(SE) p β
School Mean Individualism x School Mean Org. Support																0.42 (0.206) .043		10%	0.44 (0.221) .050 0.05
School Mean Collectivism x School Mean Org. Support																0.13 (0.381) .740		17%	0.02 (0.374) .951 0.002
Principal External Accountability Toward Management																			0.16 (0.046) .001 0.07

Random Part	Variance	Variance	Expl. variance	Variance	Expl. variance	Variance	Expl. variance	Variance	Expl. variance	Variance	Expl. variance	Variance	Expl. variance	Variance	Expl. variance
σ_e^2	0.350	0.349	0.03%	0.317	9%	0.317	9%	0.317	9%	0.316	10%	0.316	10%	0.317	9%
$\sigma_{u_0}^2$	0.110	0.112	0	0.115	0	0.114	0	0.114	0	0.094	15%	0.091	17%	0.078	29%

Note: [a] School size was divided by 1,000.

Notes

1 A list of missing values on the item level can be obtained from the authors on request.
2 A few additional variables were included in the questionnaire but were excluded from the analyses because of low reliability (power distance and uncertainty avoidance) or for theoretical reasons (teachers' and principals' job autonomy).
3 Retrieved on March 29th 2020 15.15–15.20 from www.hofstede-insights.com/product/compare-countries/
4 We did not choose to include institutional collectivism, given its definition: the degree to which organizational and societal institutional practices encourage and reward collective distribution of resources and collective action.
5 These plots are available from the authors on request.
6 These plots are available from the authors on request.

4 Study findings

Joris G.J. Beek, Zehava Rosenblatt, and Theo Wubbels

Introduction

In this chapter, we present the findings across and within countries. We report on teachers and principals, findings on the distribution of accountability (external and internal with regard to two audiences, parents and school management), and the distribution of cultural values (individualism and collectivism) and organizational support. Then we move to the findings on the prediction of teachers' accountability by cultural values and organizational support. Finally, we present a summary of all findings on predictions of teachers' and principals' accountability.

These topics were investigated using a questionnaire that included scales representing the main study variables. Scale items were answered on a five-point Likert scale (ranging from 1 to 5) and, per scale, an average score was created for all items together also ranging from 1–5. The study sample included 2,554 teachers from eight countries and 132 principals from six countries. More details about the study samples, population, and data collection can be found in Chapter 3 – Study Methods. The principals selected for the study matched the teachers' sample, so that each principal could be identified by their respective teachers in the same school. The number of principals in each school and each country varied. The across and within country tests met the minimum sample size requirements, but for some countries the distribution of principals' scores between males and females was not close to equal. It should be noted that both the samples of *South Africa* and *Zimbabwe* included a relatively small number of male principals. This combined with the small within countries sample sizes made us cautious about inferences concerning the observed within country principal variations in these countries. We used hierarchical linear modeling (HLM) to analyze the teacher data and simple regressions to analyze the principal data. We present effect size statistics according to Cohens' (1988) criteria.

Accountability distribution

In this section, we describe external and internal accountability dispositions across countries and according to the teachers' and principals' gender and seniority (number of years working as a teacher or principal).

Accountability across countries

Accountability disposition mean distribution

Tables 4.1 and 4.2 present scale means and standard deviations (SDs) for the two study samples (teachers and principals, respectively), as well as for the participating eight (teachers) or six (principals) countries. Tests of the difference between the two accountability dimensions are presented in the two tables as well. Also, a graphic representation of the country mean scores is portrayed in Figures 4.1 and 4.2. Results showed that

Table 4.1 Teachers' Accountability: Means and Standard Deviations of Accountability, T-Tests, and Effect Sizes for Comparison of External and Internal Accountability

	N	External M (SD)	Internal M (SD)	T-Tests Comparison Accountability Dispositions	Effect Size (Cohen's d)
Canada	169	3.80 (0.55)	4.57 (0.41)	$t(168)=-19.18$, $p<.001$	1.60
China	266	3.66 (0.58)	4.25 (0.56)	$t(265)=-16.11$, $p<.001$	1.03
Hungary	338	3.90 (0.54)	4.57 (0.39)	$t(337)=-24.27$, $p<.001$	1.42
Israel	418	4.11 (0.53)	4.63 (0.46)	$t(417)=-22.03$, $p<.001$	1.04
Netherlands	178	3.62 (0.44)	4.06 (0.45)	$t(177)=-13.57$, $p<.001$	0.97
South Africa	315	4.13 (0.49)	4.67 (0.39)	$t(314)=-22.10$, $p<.001$	1.22
Spain	470	3.68 (0.59)	4.38 (0.48)	$t(469)=-27.17$, $p<.001$	1.31
Zimbabwe	400	4.10 (0.52)	4.49 (0.48)	$t(399)=-13.38$, $p<.001$	0.76
Total	2554	3.90 (0.57)	4.47 (0.49)	$t(2,553)=-54.06$, $p<.001$	1.07

76 Study findings

Table 4.2 Principals' Accountability: Means and Standard Deviations of Accountability, T-Tests, and Effect Sizes for Comparison of External and Internal Accountability

	N	External	Internal	T-Tests Comparison Accountability Dispositions	Effect Size (Cohen's d)
Hungary	23	4.14 (0.34)	4.63 (0.42)	$t(22)=-4.99$, $p<.001$	1.29
Israel	30	4.31 (0.35)	4.67 (0.34)	$t(29)=-7.54$, $p<.001$	1.04
Netherlands	21	3.78 (0.51)	4.12 (0.39)	$t(20)=-4.71$, $p<.001$	0.74
South Africa	17	4.31 (0.37)	4.83 (0.24)	$t(16)=-5.30$, $p<.001$	1.67
Spain	21	4.12 (0.53)	4.49 (0.46)	$t(20)=-3.76$, $p=.001$	0.76
Zimbabwe	20	4.46 (0.52)	4.75 (0.33)	$t(19)=-3.39$, $p=.003$	0.66
Total	132	4.19 (0.48)	4.58 (0.43)	$t(131)=-11.69$, $p<.001$	0.86

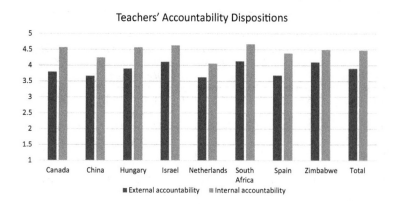

Figure 4.1 Teachers' External and Internal Accountability by Country

teacher country means for external accountability varied between 3.62 (SD=0.44, *the Netherlands*) and 4.13 (SD=0.49, *South Africa*), while for internal accountability teacher means varied between 4.06 (SD=0.46, *the Netherlands*) and 4.67 (SD=0.39, *South Africa*). Principals' results show that country means for external accountability varied between 3.78 (SD=0.51, *the Netherlands*) and 4.46 (SD=0.52, *Zimbabwe*) while for

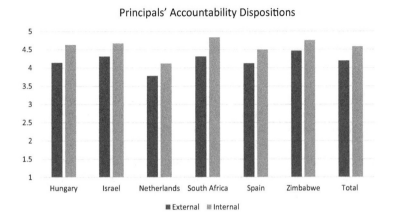

Figure 4.2 Principals' External and Internal Accountability by Country

internal accountability means varied between 4.12 (SD=0.39, *the Netherlands*) and 4.83 (SD=0.24, *South Africa*).

We tested the difference between external and internal accountability scores and the comparison of the two accountability dimensions showed that *teachers'* internal accountability was significantly higher than their external accountability for the total sample ($t(2,553)=-54.06$, $p < .001$) as well as for every individual country. Also, the *principals'* internal accountability was across-the-board significantly higher than their external accountability for the total sample ($t(131)=-11.69$. $p < .001$) as well as for each individual country. Effect sizes of the differences were large in every country. The identical trends in all countries in regard to the gap between external and internal accountability as well as to the significance and size of the differences between the two accountability types are striking. These results indicate that, although teachers and principals on average saw themselves accountable both externally and internally, they largely preferred the internal, professional standards over the external ones, namely, they tended more to report according to their own professional and ethical codes rather than to their superior's set standards.

Accountability similarities and differences among countries

Based on the accountability mean scores provided previously, we performed additional analyses to find out to what extent countries differed from each other with regard to the teachers' and principals' accountability variables.

78 Study findings

We tested whether the differences between the country means were significant by conducting Multivariate Analysis of Variance (MANOVAs), including Bonferroni post hoc tests.[1]

TEACHERS

Results showed a significant difference between accountability means of the countries for teachers' external accountability scores ($F(7, 2546)=51.54$; $p < .001$; partial $\eta^2=.124$) and for teachers' internal accountability scores ($F(7, 2546)=51.14$; $p < .001$; partial $\eta^2=.123$), meaning that there are country means that differed from one another. The partial η^2 score represents the explained variance according to country: 12.4% for external accountability and 12.3% for internal accountability. These can be considered medium effect sizes.

It is possible to form clusters of countries where teachers scored similarly on the accountability dispositions. In regard to external accountability for teachers (Table 4.3), counting from highest scoring countries to lowest, *South Africa, Israel,* and *Zimbabwe* can be grouped as the countries with high teacher external accountability that significantly differed from *Canada, Spain, China,* and *the Netherlands* (the lowest cluster), and from *Hungary* (middle). Another clustering formation was to group *Hungary* and *Canada* together as a middle-score cluster, significantly different than each other country. When grouping countries from highest to lowest scores on teachers' internal accountability (Table 4.4), a slightly different order and grouping appeared than for teachers' external accountability. *South Africa, Israel, Canada,* and *Hungary* had the highest mean score cluster, significantly higher than each other country. *Canada, Hungary,* and *Zimbabwe* also form a cluster of average scores; a cluster that is significantly higher or lower compared to each of the other countries.

Table 4.3 Country Similarities and Differences on Teachers' External Accountability

Country	South Africa	Israel	Zimbabwe	Hungary	Canada	Spain	China	Netherlands
M	4.13	4.11	4.10	3.90	3.80	3.68	3.66	3.62
(SD)	(0.49)	(0.53)	(0.52)	(0.54)	(0.55)	(0.59)	(0.58)	(0.44)

Note: A straight line under the country groups refers to similar (non-significant different) country means.

Table 4.4 Country Similarities and Differences on Teachers' Internal Accountability

Country	South Africa	Israel	Canada	Hungary	Zimbabwe	Spain	China	Netherlands
M	4.67	4.63	4.57	4.57	4.49	4.38	4.25	4.06
(SD)	(0.39)	(0.46)	(0.41)	(0.39)	(0.48)	(0.48)	(0.56)	(0.45)

Note: A straight line under the country groups refers to similar (non-significant different) country means.

Table 4.5 Country Similarities and Differences on Principals' External Accountability

Country	Zimbabwe	Israel	South Africa	Hungary	Spain	Netherlands
M	4.46	4.31	4.31	4.14	4.12	3.78
(SD)	(0.52)	(0.35)	(0.37)	(0.34)	(0.53)	(0.51)

Note: A straight line under the country groups refers to similar (non-significant different) country means.

PRINCIPALS

The MANOVA for each of the accountability types for principals also showed differences between country means in both dimensions (external accountability, $F(5, 126)=6.12$, $p < .001$; partial $\eta^2=.195$; internal accountability, $F(5,126)=9.61$, $p < .001$; partial $\eta^2=.276$). As for principals' external accountability (Table 4.5), we found two clustering formations. The first formation included two clusters: *Zimbabwe, Israel*, and *South Africa* formed the higher cluster, while *Hungary, Spain*, and *the Netherlands* consisted of the lower cluster. The second formation had all countries except *the Netherlands* – the lowest country – in one cluster. Clustering of principals' internal accountability (Table 4.6) was identical to the second formation in principals' external clustering – *the Netherlands* came up as lowest in internal accountability.

Gender and accountability

Looking at gender differences in external and internal accountability for *teachers* (Tables 4.7 and 4.8), findings showed that in the total sample female teachers scored slightly and significantly higher than males on the two accountability scales. However, the effect sizes of these differences were small. Within countries generally females also scored higher than

Table 4.6 Country Similarities and Differences on Principals' Internal Accountability

Country	South Africa	Zimbabwe	Israel	Hungary	Spain	Netherlands
M	4.83	4.75	4.67	4.63	4.49	4.12
(SD)	(0.24)	(0.33)	(0.34)	(0.42)	(0.46)	(0.39)

Note: A straight line under the country groups refers to similar (non-significant different) country means.

Table 4.7 *Teacher* Gender Differences for External Accountability, Means, Standard Deviations, T-Tests, and Effect Sizes

	External Accountability			
	Female (SD)	Male (SD)	T-Test Comparison Female vs Male	Effect Size (Cohen's d)
Canada	3.77 (0.55)	3.86 (0.55)	$t(167)=-0.93$, $p=.352$	0.15
China	3.70 (0.58)	3.59 (0.58)	$t(264)=1.46$, $p=.146$	0.19
Hungary	3.92 (0.53)	3.82 (0.57)	$t(336)=1.35$, $p=.178$	0.18
Israel	4.13 (0.51)	4.05 (0.57)	$t(416)=1.33$, $p=.184$	0.14
Netherlands	3.59 (0.49)	3.65 (0.39)	$t(176)=-0.77$, $p=.441$	0.12
South Africa	4.11 (0.50)	4.17 (0.48)	$t(313)=-0.77$, $p=.441$	0.11
Spain	3.70 (0.58)	3.66 (0.60)	$t(468)=0.61$, $p=.545$	0.06
Zimbabwe	4.13 (0.56)	4.08 (0.47)	$t(398)=0.98$, $p=.327$	0.10
Total	**3.93** (0.57)	**3.86** (0.57)	$t(2552)=3.00$, $p=.003$	0.13

Note: Means of significant different values are **bold** ($p < .05$).

males, but nearly all differences were insignificant. That is to say, females somewhat more than males felt accountable both externally and internally with the exception of *Canada, the Netherlands,* and *South Africa* for external accountability, where the opposite was true (males were somewhat higher) and *Canada* for internal accountability, where accountability levels were equal. Only *Zimbabwe* women scored significantly lower than *Zimbabwe* men on internal accountability.

Table 4.8 Teacher Gender Differences for Internal Accountability, Means, Standard Deviations, T-Tests, and Effect Sizes

	Internal Accountability			
	Female M (SD)	Male M (SD)	T-Test Comparison Female vs Male	Effect Size (Cohen's d)
Canada	4.61 (0.43)	4.51 (0.36)	$t(167)=1.62$, $p=.107$	0.27
China	4.24 (0.61)	4.26 (0.47)	$t(237.2)=-0.28$, $p=.783$[a]	0.03
Hungary	4.57 (0.38)	4.55 (0.43)	$t(336)=0.38$, $p=.702$	0.05
Israel	4.65 (0.44)	4.56 (0.51)	$t(416)=1.75$, $p=.081$	0.18
Netherlands	4.06 (0.49)	4.06 (0.43)	$t(176)=-0.01$, $p=.994$	0.001
South Africa	4.67 (0.39)	4.66 (0.38)	$t(313)=0.29$, $p=.771$	0.04
Spain	4.42 (0.45)	4.34 (0.50)	$t(468)=1.72$, $p=.086$	0.16
Zimbabwe	**4.53** (0.44)	**4.43** (0.51)	$t(365.46)=2.05$, $p=.041$[a]	0.21
Total	**4.51** (0.48)	**4.40** (0.50)	$t(2552)=5.6$, $p<.001$	0.23

Note: [a] Levene's Test for Equality of Variances $p < .05$; means of significant different values are **bold** ($p < .05$).

Tables 4.9 and 4.10 present *principals'* results by gender in the total sample and respective countries. Similar to the teachers' case, female principals scored higher than males on external accountability, although no gender difference was found for internal accountability. Within countries, no significant differences were found between male and female principals' scores on accountability types, which may be a result of the low power of the test because of the small samples.

Seniority and accountability

Regarding the relations between teacher and principal seniority and accountability dispositions (see Table 4.11), we saw no significant correlation between *teachers'* seniority and external accountability for the total sample, although we did see a significant relation between internal accountability and teacher seniority. As for individual countries, for *South Africa* teachers, we found a significant correlation between seniority and both accountability

82 *Study findings*

Table 4.9 Principal Gender Differences for External Accountability, Means, Standard Deviations, T-Tests, and Effect Size

	External Accountability			
	Female M (SD)	Male M (SD)	T-Test Comparison Female vs Male	Effect Size (Cohen's d)
Hungary	4.16 (0.22)	4.12 (0.42)	$t(21)$=0.25, p=.803	0.11
Israel	4.32 (0.39)	4.29 (0.30)	$t(28)$=0.22, p=.828	0.09
Netherlands	3.82 (0.46)	3.76 (0.54)	$t(19)$=0.22, p=.826	0.11
South Africa	4.35 (0.35)	4.13 (0.48)	$t(15)$=0.91, p=.377	0.52
Spain	4.24 (0.48)	3.99 (0.57)	$t(19)$=1.09, p=.289	0.47
Zimbabwe	4.40 (0.54)	4.70 (0.39)	$t(18)$=−1.03, p=.317	0.63
Total	**4.27** (0.44)	**4.08** (0.51)	$t(130)$=2.23, p=.027	0.39

Note: Means of (marginal) significant different values are **bold** ($p < .05$).

Table 4.10 Principal Gender Differences for Internal Accountability, Means, Standard Deviations, T-Tests, and Effect Size

	Internal Accountability			
	Female M (SD)	Male M (SD)	T-Test Comparison Female vs Male	Effect Size (Cohen's d)
Hungary	4.57 (0.35)	4.68 (0.47)	$t(21)$=−0.63, p=.537	0.27
Israel	4.67 (0.35)	4.68 (0.33)	$t(28)$=−0.06, p=.953	0.02
Netherlands	4.21 (0.32)	4.07 (0.43)	$t(19)$=0.73, p=.472	0.36
South Africa	4.81 (0.26)	4.93 (0.06)	$t(15)$=−0.83, p=.419	0.68
Spain	4.47 (0.39)	4.52 (0.54)	$t(19)$=−0.21, p=.838	0.09
Zimbabwe	4.73 (0.34)	4.84 (0.33)	$t(18)$=−0.57, p=.577	0.32
Total	4.62 (0.37)	4.52 (0.50)	$t(91.36)$=1.36, p=.178[a]	0.25

Note: [a] Levene's Test for Equality of Variances $p < .05$.

Table 4.11 Correlations Between Teacher and Principal Seniority and Accountability

Country	Teachers External Accountability	Teachers Internal Accountability	Principals External Accountability	Principals Internal Accountability
Canada	−.041	−.01		
China	−.082	.056		
Hungary	.080	.008	.427*	.051
Israel	.048	.028	−.190	.010
Netherlands	.161*	.024	−.463*	−.169
South Africa	.212*	.127*	.279	.191
Spain	.006	.076	.094	.120
Zimbabwe	.050	.058	.603**	.566**
Total	.029	.068**	.001	−.017

Note: * $p < .05$, ** $p < .01$.

types. For *the Netherlands*, we only found a significant correlation between seniority and external accountability. All effect sizes were small.

Within the total sample of *principals*, no relation was found between seniority and any of the accountability dispositions. Examining specific countries, *Hungary* (r(23)=.427, p=.042) and *Zimbabwe* (r(20)=.603, p=.005) showed a positive relation between seniority and principals' external accountability. For *Zimbabwe*, a similar positive marginally significant relation is seen within the relation between principals' internal accountability and seniority (r(20)=.566, p=.009). Principals from *the Netherlands* have a negative relation between their seniority and external accountability (r(21)=−.463, p=.035).

Accountability audiences: parents and school management

In this section, we look more in depth into teachers' and principals' external accountability dispositions toward two key audiences: parents and school management (in the case of principals it would be the school board). Because the number of countries included in the teacher sample was larger than in the principal sample (eight and six, respectively), only the smaller sample was used in those cases when teachers and principals were compared.

As specified in Chapter 3 – Study Methods (p. 29), we used a short measure of external accountability fitted to each of the specific audiences. Items of this measure were selected from the larger scale used in the present study. To verify content validity of the shorter audience-focused scales, we first looked into the interrelations between the full external accountability

84 *Study findings*

Table 4.12 Correlations of Accountability Toward Parents and School Management and General External Accountability

General External Accountability	Accountability Toward		Correlation Between Accountability Toward Two Audiences
	Parents	School Management	
Teachers	.446**	.516**	.452**
Principals	.557**	.572**	.762**

Note: * $p < .05$; ** $p < .01$.

scale and the two shorter ones. Results (Table 4.12) showed significant correlations among all three accountability scales at medium effect size. The correlations found between the general scale and each of the small audience-focused scales for teachers and principals ranged between r=.446 and r=.572, attesting to the significant shared meaning between the general scale and the audience-specific ones, while leaving some independent meaning to each. Note that the correlation between the two audience-fitted (school management and parents) scales for principals (r=.762) was higher than that related to teachers (r=.452). This may mean that principals' distinction between the two audiences was smaller than that of teachers (see our interpretations on these preliminary correlations in Chapter 5 – Discussion of Study Findings, p. 128–129).

Teachers' accountability toward parents and school management

Teachers' accountability disposition toward parents was consistently lower than toward their school management, both for our teacher sample as a whole ($t(2,553)=-26.68$, $p < .001$) and for the individual countries (see Table 4.13 and Figure 4.3). Teachers from *the Netherlands* had the lowest accountability toward both parents (3.24(SD=0.69)) and school management (3.46(SD=0.66)). Teachers from *Spain* had the highest accountability disposition toward parents (3.88(SD=0.67)) and teachers from *Israel* (4.3(SD=0.57)) and *South Africa* (4.37(SD=0.53)) held the highest scores for their accountability disposition toward their school management. Most noteworthy were the large effect sizes of the differences between dispositions toward parents and school management for *Israel* and *South Africa*. Medium to large effect sizes were observed for *Canada* and *Zimbabwe*. The effect sizes for the different dispositions toward audiences were smaller for teachers from *Spain, China,* and *the Netherlands*. These results showed that accountability dispositions toward external audiences such as parents and school management seemed to vary across countries.

Table 4.13 Teachers' Means and Standard Deviations of Accountability Toward Parents and School Management, T-Tests, and Effect Sizes

	N	External Accountability Toward Parents	School Management	T-Test Comparison Accountability Dispositions	Effect Size (Cohen's d)
Canada	169	3.68 (0.78)	4.18 (0.56)	$t(168)=-10.71$, $p < .001$	0.74
China	266	3.61 (0.77)	3.72 (0.67)	$t(265)=-2.81$, $p = .005$	0.16
Hungary	338	3.60 (0.73)	3.89 (0.63)	$t(337)=-8.09$, $p < .001$	0.43
Israel	418	3.62 (0.80)	4.37 (0.57)	$t(417)=-18.85$, $p < .001$	1.08
Netherlands	178	3.24 (0.69)	3.46 (0.66)	$t(177)=-4.57$, $p < .001$	0.34
South Africa	315	3.80 (0.82)	4.37 (0.53)	$t(314)=-14.74$, $p < .001$	0.83
Spain	470	3.88 (0.67)	3.96 (0.63)	$t(469)=-4.76$, $p < .001$	0.12
Zimbabwe	400	3.70 (0.92)	4.30 (0.61)	$t(399)=-11.66$, $p < .001$	0.77
Total	2,554	3.68 (0.80)	4.08 (0.67)	$t(2,553)=-26.68$, $p < .001$	0.54

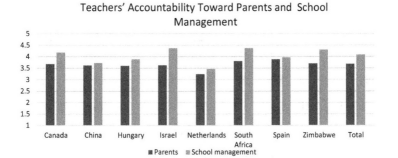

Figure 4.3 Teachers' External Accountability Toward Parents and School Management by Country

Principals' accountability toward parents and school management

For principals, we observed a similar effect as for teachers. Principals' accountability disposition toward school management was significantly higher than toward parents for the whole sample ($t(131)=-4.57, p < .001$) (see Table 4.14 and Figure 4.4). Similarly to teachers, *Dutch* principals scored the lowest on accountability to the two audiences: for parents (3.44(SD=0.60)) and for school management (3.50(SD=0.83)). Principals from *Spain*, similarly to *Spanish* teachers, scored highest toward parents (4.48(SD=0.47)), and *Israeli* principals scored highest toward school management (4.48(SD=0.47)). Effect sizes of the significant differences were medium size.

Comparison between teachers' and principals' accountability toward audiences

We looked into the comparison between teachers' and principals' accountability dispositions toward parents and school management. In regard to *parents* (Table 4.15 and Figure 4.5), results showed that principals' accountability

Table 4.14 Principals' Means and Standard Deviations of Accountability Toward Parents and School Management, T-Tests, and Effect Sizes

	N	External Accountability Toward Parents	School Management	T-Tests Comparison Accountability Dispositions	Effect Size (Cohen's d)
Hungary	23	4.08 (0.55)	4.21 (0.52)	$t(22)=-1.11$, $p=.277$	0.24
Israel	30	**4.09** (0.56)	**4.48** (0.47)	$t(29)=-4.55$, $p < .001$	0.75
Netherlands	21	3.44 (0.60)	3.50 (0.83)	$t(20)=-0.49$, $p=.629$	0.09
South Africa	17	**4.09** (0.62)	**4.29** (0.60)	$t(16)=-2.99$, $p=.009$	0.32
Spain	21	4.33 (0.51)	4.46 (0.51)	$t(20)=-1.64$, $p=.116$	0.26
Zimbabwe	20	4.00 (1.14)	4.19 (0.90)	$t(19)=-1.53$, $p=.143$	0.19
Total	132	**4.01** (0.72)	**4.21** (0.71)	$t(131)=-4.57$, $p < .001$	0.27

Note: Means of significant different external and internal accountability values are **bold** ($p < .05$).

Study findings 87

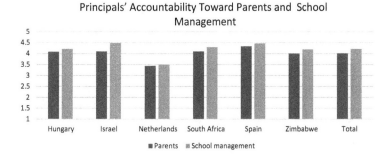

Figure 4.4 Principals' External Accountability Toward Parents and School Management by Country

Table 4.15 Teachers' and Principals' Means and Standard Deviations of Accountability Toward Parents, T-Tests, and Effect Sizes

	Teachers		_Principals_			
	N	*Accountability Score M (SD)*	N	*Accountability Score M (SD)*	*T-Test Comparison Accountability Dispositions*	*Effect Size (Cohen's d)*
Hungary	333	**3.60** (0.73)	23	**4.08** (0.55)	$t(354)=-3.10$, $p=.002$	0.75
Israel	361	**3.62** (0.80)	30	**4.09** (0.56)	$t(389)=-3.18$, $p=.002$	0.69
Netherlands	169	3.22 (0.70)	21	3.44 (0.60)	$t(188)=-1.34$, $p=.182$	0.33
South Africa	315	3.80 (0.82)	17	4.09 (0.62)	$t(330)=-1.45$, $p=.147$	0.40
Spain	318	**3.86** (0.65)	21	**4.33** (0.51)	$t(337)=-3.24$, $p=.001$	0.80
Zimbabwe	398	3.70 (0.92)	20	4.00 (1.14)	$t(416)=-1.38$, $p=.168$	0.28
Total	1894	**3.67** (0.80)	132	**4.01** (0.72)	$t(2024)=-4.74$, $p<.001$	0.45

Note: Means of significant different external and internal accountability values are **bold** ($p < .05$).

was significantly higher than teachers' accountability ($t(2024)=-4.74$, $p < .001$). This difference was observed for three individual countries: *Hungary*, *Israel*, and *Spain*. The effect sizes for the countries in which teachers and principals differed were medium (*Hungary* and *Israel*) to large (*Spain*).

88 Study findings

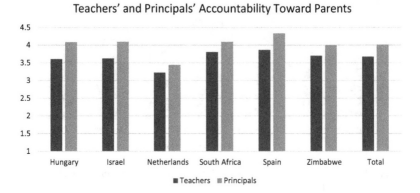

Figure 4.5 Teachers' and Principals' Accountability Toward Parents by Country

In the remaining three countries (*the Netherlands, South Africa*, and *Zimbabwe*), accountability toward parents was also higher than toward school management, but the differences were not significant.

As for *school management* (Table 4.16 and Figure 4.6), no significant difference was observed between teachers and principals in all countries together ($t(2024)=-1.6$, $p=.109$). Only two countries showed significantly higher scores for principals than teachers: *Hungary* and *Spain* (medium and large effect sizes, respectively).

To conclude, we see a trend where both teachers and principals felt more accountable toward their school management than toward their students' parents. However, when accountability preference for the two audiences was compared between samples, results showed that principals tended to be more accountable to parents than did teachers but were similar to teachers in regard to school management.

Cultural values distribution

After presenting results on our core variable accountability in the previous section, this section reports on teachers' and principals' adherence to the cultural values *individualism* and *collectivism*, used in the present study as accountability predictors. We describe differences in the two variables across countries and according to the teachers' and principals' gender and seniority (number of years working as a teacher or principal).

Table 4.16 Teachers' and Principals' Means and Standard Deviations of Accountability Toward School Management, T-Tests, and Effect Sizes

	Teachers N	Accountability M (SD)	Principals N	Accountability M (SD)	T-Test Comparison Accountability Dispositions	Effect Size (Cohen's d)
Hungary	333	**3.90** (0.63)	23	**4.21** (0.52)	$t(354)=-2.33$, $p=.021$	0.54
Israel	361	4.36 (0.58)	30	4.48 (0.47)	$t(389)=-1.07$, $p=.285$	0.22
Netherlands	169	3.46 (0.67)	21	3.50 (0.83)	$t(188)=-0.27$, $p=.787$	0.06
South Africa	315	4.37 (0.53)	17	4.29 (0.60)	$t(330)=0.62$, $p=.536$	−0.15
Spain	318	**3.89** (0.65)	21	**4.46** (0.51)	$t(337)=-3.95$, $p<.001$	0.98
Zimbabwe	398	4.30 (0.61)	20	4.19 (0.90)	$t(416)=0.74$, $p=.462$	−0.14
Total	1894	4.11 (0.67)	132	4.21 (0.71)	$t(2024)=-1.60$, $p=.109$	0.14

Note: Means of significant different external and internal accountability values are **bold** ($p < .05$).

Figure 4.6 Teachers' and Principals' Accountability Toward School Management by Country

Cultural values across countries

Cultural values mean distribution

Tables 4.17 and 4.18 present the mean scores for teachers' and principals' cultural values – individualism and collectivism – for the whole sample as well as for specific countries. Graphic representations of the country mean scores are portrayed in Figures 4.7 and 4.8. *Teachers'* mean of individualism was 3.64 (SD=0.75). Country teacher means varied between *Zimbabwe*, 3.42 (SD=0.93) and *South Africa*, 3.93 (SD=0.78). *Teachers'* collectivism mean was 4.25 (SD=0.58). Country means varied between *China*, 3.90 (SD=0.57) and *Spain*, 4.43 (SD=0.48). Comparison of the two cultural values showed that teachers' collectivism was significantly higher than their individualism for both the total sample ($t(2,553)=-33,45$, $p < .001$) and for all individual countries. The effect sizes varied between medium (e.g., *Israel*) and large (e.g., *Spain*, *Canada*, and *Zimbabwe*).

Table 4.17 Teachers' Means and Standard Deviations of Cultural Values, T-Tests, and Effect Sizes for the Comparison of Individualism and Collectivism

	N	Cultural Values Individualism	Collectivism	T-Test Comparison Cultural Values	Effect Size (Cohen's d)
Canada	169	3.80 (0.61)	4.34 (0.49)	$t(168)=-9.44$, $p<.001$	0.99
China	266	3.54 (0.63)	3.90 (0.57)	$t(265)=-7.62$, $p<.001$	0.60
Hungary	338	3.75 (0.67)	4.32 (0.54)	$t(337)=-12.28$, $p<.001$	0.93
Israel	418	3.82 (0.69)	4.20 (0.64)	$t(417)=-9.76$, $p<.001$	0.57
Netherlands	178	3.47 (0.52)	4.03 (0.46)	$t(177)=-10.06$, $p<.001$	1.13
South Africa	315	3.93 (0.78)	4.35 (0.52)	$t(314)=-7.59$, $p<.001$	0.63
Spain	470	3.48 (0.71)	4.43 (0.48)	$t(469)=-23.65$, $p<.001$	1.57
Zimbabwe	400	3.42 (0.93)	4.22 (0.65)	$t(399)=-14.67$, $p<.001$	1.00
Total	2554	3.64 (0.75)	4.25 (0.58)	$t(2,553)=-33.45$, $p<.001$	0.90

Table 4.18 Principals' Means and Standard Deviations of Cultural Values, T-Tests, and Effect Sizes for Comparison of Individualism and Collectivism

	N	Individualism	Collectivism	T-Test Comparison Cultural Values	Effect Size (Cohen's d)
Hungary	23	2.88 (0.84)	4.38 (0.46)	$t(22)=-8.07$, $p < .001$	2.20
Israel	30	3.62 (0.84)	4.35 (0.47)	$t(29)=-4.19$, $p < .001$	1.07
Netherlands	21	3.19 (0.68)	4.03 (0.40)	$t(20)=-4.24$, $p < .001$	1.49
South Africa	17	3.12 (0.92)	4.28 (0.41)	$t(16)=-4.24$, $p=.001$	1.63
Spain	21	3.72 (0.73)	2.61 (0.60)	$t(20)=7.97$, $p < .001$	−1.66
Zimbabwe	20	2.75 (1.22)	4.44 (0.54)	$t(19)=-5.04$, $p < .001$	1.79
Total	132	3.24 (0.94)	4.03 (0.79)	$t(131)=-6.73$, $p < .001$	0.91

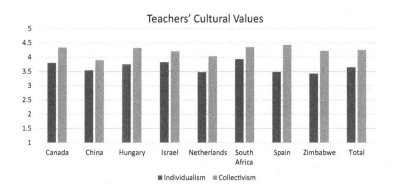

Figure 4.7 Teachers' Cultural Values by Country

Similar to the results of the teachers' data, for *principals* the individualism mean, 3.24 (SD=0.94), was lower than the general collectivism mean, 4.03 (SD=0.79) ($t(131)=-6.73, p < .001$). Principals' country means of individualism varied from *Zimbabwe*, 2.75 (SD=1.22), similar to the teachers' mean score in this country, to *Israel*, 3.62 (SD=0.84). Principals' country means of collectivism varied between *Spain*, 2.61

92 Study findings

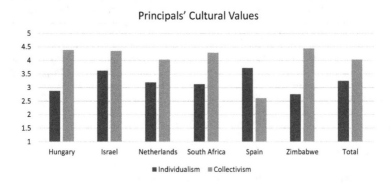

Figure 4.8 Principals' Cultural Values by Country

(SD=0.60) and *Zimbabwe*, 4.44 (SD=0.54). It is noteworthy that for *Spain* the mean of individualism, 3.72 (SD=0.73), was higher than the mean of collectivism, 2.61 (SD=0.60) ($t(20)$=7.97, $p < .001$), making *Spanish* principals the only group with a higher score for individualism than collectivism.

Cultural values – similarities and differences among countries

To explore whether the differences in cultural values among countries were significant, we used MANOVA. We next present the separate analyses for teachers and principals.

TEACHERS

MANOVA results for teachers showed a significant difference among countries in individualism ($F(7,2546)$=23.80; $p < .001$; partial η^2=.061) and collectivism scores ($F(7,2546)$=29.80; $p < .001$; partial η^2=.076), meaning that country means differed from one another. The partial η^2 represents the explained variance by the countries, which was 6.1% for individualism and 7.6% for collectivism, both with a small effect size.

When comparing the country teacher means on cultural values, individualism seemed to form two clustering formations (Table 4.19[2]). The first formation featured two distinctive groups: one consisted of the highest cluster, including *Canada, Hungary, Israel,* and *South Africa*. The other group consisted of the lowest cluster, including *China, Spain, the Netherlands,* and *Zimbabwe*. The two groups were significantly different from one another. The second formation consisted of three countries, *Israel, Canada,* and

Table 4.19 Country Similarities and Differences on Teachers' Individualism

Country	South Africa	Israel	Canada	Hungary	China	Spain	Netherlands	Zimbabwe
M	3.93	3.82	3.8	3.75	3.54	3.48	3.47	3.42
(SD)	(0.78)	(0.69)	(0.61)	(0.67)	(0.63)	(0.71)	(0.52)	(0.93)

Note: A straight line under the country groups refers to similar (non-significant different) country means.

Table 4.20 Country Similarities and Differences on Teachers' Collectivism

Country	Spain	South Africa	Canada	Hungary	Zimbabwe	Israel	Netherlands	China
M	4.43	4.35	4.34	4.32	4.22	4.20	4.03	3.90
(SD)	(0.48)	(0.52)	(0.49)	(0.54)	(0.65)	(0.64)	(0.46)	(0.57)

Note: A straight line under the country groups refers to similar (non-significant different) country means.

Hungary, forming a medium-score group that was significantly different (either higher or lower) than any other country.

Teacher collectivism (Table 4.20) seemed to form three clustering formations. The first consisted of three clusters: highest collectivism (*Spain, South Africa, Canada,* and *Hungary*), medium collectivism (*Zimbabwe* and *Israel*), and lowest collectivism (*the Netherlands* and *China*). The second formation featured *South Africa, Canada, Hungary,* and *Zimbabwe* as a lower cluster than *Spain* alone but higher than the cluster that consisted of *the Netherlands* and *China*. The third formation featured a medium-score cluster of *Canada, Hungary, Zimbabwe,* and *Israel*, which was different from each of the four other countries.

PRINCIPALS

Similar to the teacher case, results for principals showed significant country differences for individualism ($F(5,126)=4.44$, $p=.001$; partial $\eta^2=.150$) and collectivism ($F(5,126)=44.14$, $p < .001$; partial $\eta^2=.637$). A clustering analysis of country individualism showed two formations. According to one formation, *Zimbabwe* had the lowest score, significantly lower than all of the other five countries (see Table 4.21). The other formation showed that *Spain* had the highest score, significantly higher than all of the other five countries. As for collectivism (see Table 4.22), *Spain* had the lowest score, significantly different from all of the other five countries.

Table 4.21 Country Similarities and Differences on Principals' Individualism

Country	Spain	Israel	Netherlands	South Africa	Hungary	Zimbabwe
M	3.72	3.62	3.19	3.12	2.88	2.75
(SD)	(0.73)	(0.84)	(0.68)	(0.92)	(0.84)	(1.22)

Note: A straight line under the country groups refers to similar (non-significant different) country means.

Table 4.22 Country Similarities and Differences on Principals' Collectivism

Country	Zimbabwe	Hungary	Israel	South Africa	Netherlands	Spain
M	4.44	4.38	4.35	4.28	4.03	2.61
(SD)	(0.54)	(0.46)	(0.47)	(0.41)	(0.40)	(0.60)

Note: A straight line under the country groups refers to similar (non-significant different) country means.

Differences in cultural values by gender

In this section, we present scores on cultural values for the total sample as well as for the respective countries differentiated by teacher and principal gender. Tables 4.23 and 4.24 feature the cultural values individualism and collectivism by gender for teachers and Tables 4.25 and 4.26 show the cultural values for principals.

Teachers

Female teachers in the all-country sample valued both individualism and collectivism more than males. However, single country analysis showed differential scores for the two values between women and men. In regard to individualism, female *Canadian* teachers scored significantly higher than their male counterparts and *Chinese* women scored significantly lower than males. Both effect sizes in these countries were small. In *Israel* and *Zimbabwe*, female teachers scored only marginally lower than males ($t(416)=1.78$, $p=.08$, $t(389)=1.94$, $p=.05$, respectively). The differences between female and male scores in the other countries – *Hungary, the Netherlands, Spain*, and *South Africa* – were insignificant. As for collectivism, in three countries – *Hungary, Spain*, and *Zimbabwe* – female teachers scored significantly higher than male teachers with only small effect sizes. The male and female scores of the other five countries – *Canada, China, Israel, South Africa*, and *Zimbabwe* – did not differ significantly.

Table 4.23 Teacher Gender Differences for Individualism, Means, Standard Deviations, T-Tests, and Effect Sizes

	Female (SD)	Male (SD)	T-Test Comparison Female vs Male	Effect Size (Cohen's d)
Canada	**3.87** (0.55)	**3.66** (0.69)	$t(167)$=2.22, p=.028	0.35
China	**3.48** (0.66)	**3.65** (0.57)	$t(264)$=−2.11, p=.036	0.28
Hungary	3.75 (0.68)	3.72 (0.67)	$t(336)$=0.35, p=.729	0.05
Israel	3.78 (0.71)	3.91 (0.62)	$t(416)$=−1.78, p=.075	0.20
Netherlands	3.50 (0.56)	3.45 (0.49)	$t(176)$=0.63, p=.533	0.09
South Africa	3.96 (0.75)	3.82 (0.87)	$t(95.98)$=1.2, p=.235[a]	0.17
Spain	3.48 (0.7)	3.48 (0.87)	$t(468)$=0.04, p=.966	0.004
Zimbabwe	3.50 (0.91)	3.32 (0.94)	$t(398)$=1.94, p=.053	0.19
Total	**3.68** (0.74)	**3.58** (0.75)	$t(2,552)$=3.32, p=.001	0.14

Note: [a] Levene's Test for Equality of Variances $p < .05$; means of significant different values are **bold** ($p < .05$).

Table 4.24 Teacher Gender Differences for Collectivism, Means, Standard Deviations, T-Tests, and Effect Sizes

	Female (SD)	Male (SD)	T-Tests Comparison Female vs Male	Effect Size (Cohen's d)
Canada	4.38 (0.48)	4.27 (0.51)	$t(167)$=1.43, p=.155	0.23
China	3.9 (0.59)	3.9 (0.53)	$t(264)$=0.07, p=.948	0.01
Hungary	**4.35** (0.52)	**4.17** (0.61)	$t(336)$=2.46, p=.014	0.32
Israel	4.22 (0.60)	4.13 (0.71)	$t(416)$=1.32, p=.188	0.14
Netherlands	3.98 (0.51)	4.06 (0.42)	$t(176)$=−1.22, p=.226	0.18
South Africa	4.35 (0.51)	4.33 (0.56)	$t(313)$=0.28, p=.782	0.04
Spain	**4.48** (0.47)	**4.36** (0.49)	$t(468)$=2.69, p=.007	0.25
Zimbabwe	**4.29** (0.57)	**4.13** (0.72)	$t(398)$=2.51, p=.012	0.25
Total	**4.28** (0.56)	**4.18** (0.61)	$t(2,552)$=4.36, $p < .001$	0.18

Note: Means of significant different values are **bold** ($p < .05$).

Principals

Male principals tended to score higher on individualism ($t(130)$=−2.17, p=0.032) and female principals scored higher on collectivism; however, the difference was marginally significant ($t(130)$=1.79, p=0.076). We saw fewer within country differences between females and males than what we saw for teachers: these were in only two countries – *Hungary* and *Israel*. Male *Hungarian* principals scored higher than female principals on individualism, and on collectivism *Israeli* female principals scored higher than male principals.

Table 4.25 *Principal* Gender Differences for Individualism Means, Standard Deviations, T-Tests, and Effect Sizes

	Individualism			
	Female M (SD)	Male M (SD)	T-Tests Comparison Female vs Male	Effect Size (Cohen's d)
Hungary	**2.40** (0.78)	**3.26** (0.71)	$t(21)=-2.75, p=0.012$	1.15
Israel	3.67 (0.98)	3.53 (0.48)	$t(28)=0.53, p=0.603$[a]	0.18
Netherlands	2.90 (0.46)	3.34 (0.74)	$t(19)=-1.41, p=0.175$	0.70
South Africa	2.98 (0.86)	3.78 (1.07)	$t(15)=-1.41, p=0.179$	0.82
Spain	3.67 (0.58)	3.79 (0.89)	$t(19)=-0.37, p=0.716$	0.16
Zimbabwe	2.63 (1.04)	3.25 (1.91)	$t(3.46)=-0.63, p=0.567$[a]	0.41
Total	**3.10** (0.98)	**3.45** (0.85)	$t(130)=-2.17, p=0.032$	0.39

Note: [a] Levene's Test for Equality of Variances $p < .05$; means of significant different values are **bold** ($p < .05$).

Table 4.26 *Principal* Gender Differences for Collectivism Means, Standard Deviations, T-Tests, and Effect Sizes

	Collectivism			
	Female M (SD)	Male M (SD)	T-Test Comparison Female vs Male	Effect Size (Cohen's d)
Hungary	4.35 (0.53)	4.4 (0.43)	$t(21)=-0.27, p=0.790$	0.11
Israel	**4.49** (0.44)	**4.06** (0.40)	$t(28)=2.65, p=0.013$	1.04
Netherlands	4.14 (0.20)	3.97 (0.47)	$t(19)=0.93, p=0.363$	0.48
South Africa	4.29 (0.41)	4.25 (0.50)	$t(15)=0.13, p=0.897$	0.08
Spain	2.61 (0.52)	2.62 (0.72)	$t(19)=-0.01, p=0.996$	0.00
Zimbabwe	4.45 (0.50)	4.38 (0.75)	$t(18)=0.25, p=0.803$	0.12
Total	4.13 (0.77)	3.88 (0.81)	$t(130)=1.79, p=0.076$	0.31

Note: Means of significant different values are **bold** ($p < .05$).

Cultural values and seniority

The correlations of both cultural values with seniority for teachers and principals are shown in Table 4.27. None of the single country correlations for teachers were significant. Only the total teacher sample correlations of seniority and the two cultural values were positively significant and for principals the correlation was negative with collectivism. This was caused by a large effect in *Spain* for principals. The longer principals in *Spain* were in the job, the less they adhered to collectivist values.

Study findings 97

Table 4.27 Correlations Between Teacher and Principal Seniority and Cultural Values

Country	Teachers		Principals	
	Individualism	Collectivism	Individualism	Collectivism
Canada	.034	−.138		
China	.098	−.092		
Hungary	.066	−.031	−.140	.081
Israel	.050	.056	.009	−.121
Netherlands	−.070	−.077	−.198	.094
South Africa	−.040	−.013	−.268	−.017
Spain	.072	.079	−.317	−.608**
Zimbabwe	.046	.047	−.179	.226
Total	.047*	.061**	−.062	−.447**

Note: * $p < .05$, ** $p < .01$.

Organizational support distribution

This section presents the descriptive results for the teachers' and principals' experience of organizational support. We report results across countries as well as results pertaining to single countries, all by gender and seniority.

Organizational support across countries

In this section, we report on teachers' and principals' perception of organizational support. We present means and SDs, country differences and similarities, and background variables' (gender and seniority) differences in organizational support. The respondents' reference of supporting institution is the school in the case of teachers and the school board in the principals' case.

Organizational support mean distribution

Tables 4.28 and 4.29 show teachers' mean scores for organizational support, respectively, for the whole sample and the individual countries differentiated by gender. Figure 4.9 presents a graphic representation of the country means. The sample mean for *teachers'* organizational support was 3.64 (SD=0.78). Country means varied from *China*, 2.80 (SD=0.75) to *Canada*, 4.00 (SD=0.65). Apparently, teachers' perception of being supported by their schools was moderately high with no great variation among countries. The sample mean for *principals'* organizational support was 3.52 (SD=0.92). Country means varied from *Spain*, 2.24 (SD=0.71) to *South*

98 Study findings

Table 4.28 Teachers' Means and Standard Deviations of Organizational Support by Gender, T-Tests, and Effect Sizes

	Organizational Support				
	Total (SD)	Female (SD)	Male (SD)	T-Test Comparison Female vs Male	Effect Size (Cohen's d)
Canada	4.00 (0.65)	3.99 (0.66)	4.02 (0.64)	$t(167)=-0.31$, $p=.757$	0.05
China	2.80 (0.75)	2.78 (0.74)	2.84 (0.75)	$t(264)=-0.54$, $p=.587$	0.07
Hungary	3.90 (0.74)	3.89 (0.73)	3.92 (0.78)	$t(336)=-0.22$, $p=.827$	0.03
Israel	3.88 (0.77)	3.87 (0.72)	3.92 (0.87)	$t(416)=-0.67$, $p=.505$	0.07
Netherlands	3.59 (0.69)	3.62 (0.67)	3.56 (0.72)	$t(176)=0.59$, $p=.557$	0.09
South Africa	3.81 (0.77)	3.78 (0.75)	3.91 (0.84)	$t(313)=-1.25$, $p=.213$	0.17
Spain	3.53 (0.70)	3.52 (0.68)	3.55 (0.72)	$t(468)=-0.52$, $p=.601$	0.05
Zimbabwe	3.61 (0.76)	3.63 (0.75)	3.59 (0.78)	$t(398)=0.48$, $p=.634$	0.05
Total	3.64 (0.80)	3.66 (0.79)	3.62 (0.83)	$t(2552)=1.06$, $p=.288$	0.04

Table 4.29 Principals' Means and Standard Deviations of Organizational Support by Gender, T-Tests, and Effect Sizes

	Organizational Support				
	Total (SD)	Female (SD)	Male (SD)	T-Test Comparison Female vs Male	Effect Size (Cohen's d)
Hungary	3.60 (0.84)	3.32 (0.97)	3.82 (0.68)	$t(21)=-1.47$, $p=0.157$	0.60
Israel	3.85 (0.59)	3.89 (0.67)	3.78 (0.42)	$t(26.49)=0.53$, $p=0.598$	0.19
Netherlands	3.47 (0.86)	3.36 (0.93)	3.52 (0.85)	$t(19)=-0.41$, $p=0.685$	0.19
South Africa	3.97 (0.57)	3.99 (0.61)	3.89 (0.38)	$t(15)=0.26$, $p=0.795$	0.19
Spain	2.24 (0.71)	2.26 (0.66)	2.22 (0.80)	$t(19)=0.13$, $p=0.899$	0.06
Zimbabwe	3.93 (0.77)	3.84 (0.81)	4.29 (0.50)	$t(18)=-1.05$, $p=0.309$	0.67
Total	3.52 (0.92)	3.55 (0.93)	3.48 (0.92)	$t(130)=0.42$, $p=0.678$	0.07

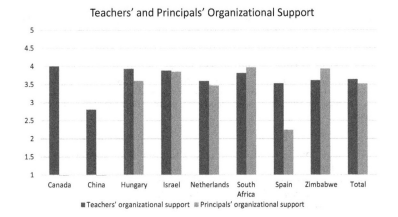

Figure 4.9 Teachers' and Principals' Organizational Support by Country

Africa, 3.97 (SD=0.57). Similar to teachers' perception of being supported by their schools, principals also perceived moderately high support from their boards, with the exception of *Spain*.

Organizational support similarities and differences among countries

To compare the *teacher* country means of organizational support, we performed an analysis of variance (ANOVA, $F(7,2546)=71.24; p < .001$; partial $\eta^2=.164$). Looking at the partial η^2, countries explained 16.4% of the variance of organizational support. Table 4.30 features the comparative scores. Similar scores were found for teachers from *Canada, Hungary, Israel*, and *South Africa*. These countries formed a cluster that was significantly higher than the next group, consisting of *the Netherlands, Spain*, and *Zimbabwe*. *China* was an exception – significantly lower than the other two clusters with a country mean 2.80 (SD=0.75).

Results for ANOVAs for *principals'* country mean scores also showed significant differences ($F(5,126)=16.92, p < .001$, partial $\eta^2=.402$). Table 4.31 shows all scores compared to each other. Similar to the case of collectivism, principals from *Spain* scored lowest on perceived organizational support and differed from all other country means.

Organizational support by gender and seniority

T-tests did not show any difference between male and female *teachers'* experience of organizational support, either for the whole sample or for

Table 4.30 Country Similarities and Differences on *Teachers'* Organizational Support

Country	Canada	Hungary	Israel	South Africa	Zimbabwe	Netherlands	Spain	China
M	4.00	3.90	3.88	3.81	3.61	3.59	3.53	2.80
(SD)	(0.65)	(0.74)	(0.77)	(0.77)	(0.76)	(0.69)	(0.70)	(0.75)

Note: A straight line under the country groups refers to similar (non-significant different) country means.

Table 4.31 Country Similarities and Differences on *Principals'* Organizational Support

Country	South Africa	Zimbabwe	Israel	Hungary	Netherlands	Spain
M	3.97	3.93	3.85	3.6	3.47	2.24
(SD)	(0.57)	(0.77)	(0.59)	(0.84)	(0.86)	(0.71)

Note: A straight line under the country groups refers to similar (non-significant different) country means.

individual countries (see Table 4.28). For *principals'* experienced organizational support, we also did not find differences according to principals' gender (see Table 4.29). Like teachers, male and female principals showed no different perception of their support from their board.

We tested the relation of seniority to teachers' and principals' organizational support with correlations shown in Table 4.32. Overall, the more experienced that *teachers* were, the more they felt supported by their school principals, although this was a small but significant effect. Among individual

Table 4.32 Correlations Between Teachers' and Principals' Seniority and Organizational Support

Country	Teachers	Principals
Canada	−.097	
China	−.077	
Hungary	.103	.031
Israel	.016	−.238
Netherlands	.040	.238
South Africa	.115*	.295
Spain	.032	−.602**
Zimbabwe	−.007	.133
Total	.078**	−.317**

Note: * $p < .05$, ** $p < .01$.

countries, only *South Africa* showed this relation. For *principals*, the relation between organizational support and seniority was negative. The longer principals were in their job, the less they felt supported by their board. This finding seemed to be slanted by *Spain*, where a similar negative finding was found.

Prediction of teachers' and principals' external and internal accountability

In this section. we present findings where we predict teachers' and principals' accountability dispositions by cultural values, perceived organizational support, and background variables. For the prediction of teacher accountability, we also added principals' accountability disposition as an additional predicting variable. Whereas the teacher models without principals' accountability dispositions were calculated for eight countries, the models that included principals' dispositions were calculated for six countries (*Canada* and *China* did not provide principal data). We first describe the teacher models: external and internal accountability without and with principal accountability contribution, and audience-focused external accountability referring to parents and school management. Then we present the principal models.

Prediction of teachers' accountability

Relationships between model variables

We first ran correlations to explore the relations among the study variables: teachers' external and internal accountability dispositions, cultural values (individualism and collectivism), and perceived organizational support (Table 4.33). We also included personal background variables (gender, seniority) and school size.

It should be noted that although the correlation between the two teacher accountability dimensions was substantial (r=.504, $p < .001$), suggesting that the two shared common content (variance), these dimensions were still far from identical: 75% of the variance attested to differences between the two. Both external and internal accountability were each significantly and positively related to the two cultural values individualism and collectivism, with small and medium effect sizes, respectively. Organizational support correlated significantly and positively with the two accountability dimensions with a medium effect size. In regard to background variables, seniority was significantly and positively related to internal accountability with a rather small effect size. Gender was significantly but negatively related to internal accountability only, meaning that females were more internally

Table 4.33 Correlations Between Teacher Study Variables

	1	2	3	4	5	6	7	8
(1) Gender	–							
(2) Seniority	.003	–						
(3) External accountability	−.059**	.029						
(4) Internal accountability	−.110**	.068**	.504**					
(5) Individualism	−.066**	.047*	.060**	.124**				
(6) Collectivism	−.086**	.061**	.282**	.369**	.075**			
(7) Organizational support	−.021	.078**	.366**	.298**	.075**	.347**		
(8) School size	.046*	−.105**	−.040*	−.107**	−.035	−.154**	−.252**	

Note: * $p < .05$; ** $p < .01$; Gender: 0=Female, 1=Male.

accountable than males. The relation of school size to internal accountability was significantly negative, again with a small effect size. These correlations paved the way to more advanced analyses of the relationships among the study variables by building multilevel multiple linear regression models for predicting teacher external and internal accountability.

Modeling teachers' accountability

In Chapter 3 – Study Methods (p. 32), we explained the need for a multilevel approach because our teacher data had a hierarchical structure in which teachers were nested within schools and within countries. Because of the small number of countries where teacher data were collected (eight) at the highest level, a two-level model was chosen over a three-level model. The final study model then included variables representing the individual teacher (first level) and those representing the school (teacher faculty) (second level).

To test for the need to consider the data's nested structure, we calculated the ICC between the two levels, i.e., the proportion of variance at the teacher and at the school levels. These ICCs showed that significant amounts of variance were located at the school level. For external accountability, 19.3% of the variance was located at the school level and for internal accountability, 20.4%. These results confirmed the leveled structure and the need for multilevel analyses.

We performed multilevel regression analyses including teacher variables and school variables as predictors. To create school scores, we aggregated the scores on the individual teacher level and used the average school teachers' score. This procedure was performed for the accountability, cultural values, and organizational support variables. Based on preliminary tests, we also included interactions between the cultural values (individualism and collectivism) and organizational support. In regard to background variables, we included gender and seniority at the individual level and school size (student body size) at the school level. When the model included principals' data (collected from six, not eight, countries), we considered principals' accountability dispositions as a school level variable.

A relation between school level variables and each of the accountability dispositions should be interpreted at the school level. The *teachers' school mean score* of, e.g., school-level individualism can only predict *the school mean* of teachers' accountability dispositions. Regression coefficients are provided that give information about individual teachers compared to their school mean. So, positive coefficients mean that teachers with a higher score for that predictor showed a higher accountability disposition compared to their within school colleagues.

Table 4.34 shows the models for predicting external and internal accountability without principals' accountability dispositions. We discuss the statistical model of external accountability followed by the statistical model predicting internal accountability.

EXTERNAL ACCOUNTABILITY RESULTS

At the teacher level, teachers' collectivism (β=0.12, $t(2,540)$=9.866, $p <$ .001) and organizational (school) support (β=0.16, $t(2,540)$=10.814, $p <$ .001) were positive significant predictors of teachers' external accountability disposition. The more teachers adhered to collectivistic views and the more they experienced organizational support, the higher their external accountability disposition. All other variables did not predict teachers' external accountability. Of the two predictors at the teacher level, organizational support had a larger standardized coefficient than collectivism, meaning that organizational support had a slightly larger predictive value. There was no significant interaction effect between collectivism and organizational support; thus, the regression coefficients for collectivism were similar for teachers across the whole range of organizational support.

The other cultural value, individualism, did not predict teachers' external accountability. Similarly, the interaction between individualism and organizational support did not predict teachers' external accountability disposition. It should be noted that the *p*-value of seniority at the individual level suggested a marginal positive relation (β=0.02, $t(2,540)$=1.696, p=.09). We also observed a marginal positive teacher level interaction between

104 *Study findings*

Table 4.34 Models for Predicting Teachers' External and Internal Accountability

	External Accountability		Internal Accountability	
	B(SE)	β	B(SE)	β
Fixed Part				
Intercept	3.91 (0.022)		4.49 (0.017)	
Gender	−0.03 (0.023)	−0.01	−0.04 (0.018)	−0.02*
Seniority	0.002 (0.001)	0.02†	0.001 (0.001)	0.01
Individualism	−0.0003 (0.014)	−0.0003	0.03 (0.014)	0.02*
Collectivism	0.21 (0.021)	0.12***	0.23 (0.018)	0.13***
Organizational support	0.20 (0.018)	0.16***	0.08 (0.014)	0.07***
Org. support x individualism	0.01 (0.018)	0.005	−0.000003 (0.017)	−0.000002
Org. support x collectivism	0.04 (0.025)	0.03†	−0.01 (0.022)	−0.005
School size (student body/1,000)	0.04 (0.034)	0.03	0 (0.025)	0.002
School mean individualism	0.10 (0.058)	0.03	0.15 (0.045)	0.05**
School mean collectivism	0.10 (0.084)	0.03***	0.27 (0.077)	0.07**
School mean org. support	0.27 (0.064)	0.12	0.16 (0.042)	0.07***
School mean individualism x school mean org. support	−0.17 (0.136)	−0.03	0.05 (0.081)	0.008
School mean collectivism x school mean org. support	−0.03 (0.11)	−0.01	−0.13 (0.073)	−0.03†
Random Part	Variance	Explained Variance	Variance	Explained Variance
σ_e^2	0.228	15%	0.167	13%
$\sigma_{u_0}^2$	0.045	30%	0.023	53%

Note: † $p < .1$, * $p < .05$, ** $p < .01$, *** $p < .001$; Gender: 0=Female, 1=Male.

teachers' collectivism and organizational support (β=0.03, $t(2,540)$=1.766, p=.08). This means that the higher teachers' collectivist views were, the stronger the relation between teachers' organizational support and their external accountability.

At the teacher school level, similar to the individual level predictors, the teachers' school mean of organizational support (β=0.13, t(178)=5.452, $p < .001$) positively predicted the school mean of teachers' external accountability: the more teachers on average felt organizational support at their work, the more they felt externally accountable. School mean of collectivism was a significant predictor of external accountability, but individualism was not, nor was there any interaction. School size had no relation to external accountability. These results showed that the teachers' individualistic, collectivistic, and organizational support characteristics predicted external accountability to a stronger degree than personal characteristics.

The model explained 15% of the variance on the teacher level and 30% on the school level. The total explained variance of the model was 18%, so about one-fifth of the variance between teachers' external accountability scores is explained by the predictors both at the teacher and school levels.

INTERNAL ACCOUNTABILITY RESULTS

Similar to the external accountability model, both teachers' collectivism (β=0.13, t(2,540)=12.739, $p < .001$) and organizational support (β=0.07, t(2,540)=5.989, $p < .001$) were positive significant predictors at the teacher level for internal accountability. The other cultural value, individualism (β=0.02, t(2,540)=2.028, p=.042) showed to be a positive significant predictor as well. Gender turned out to be the only significant background predictor (β=−0.02, t(2,540)=−2.376, p=.018). The negative sign meant that female teachers felt more accountable than their male counterparts. Both interactions between organizational support and the cultural values were not significant predictors.

At the school level, all variables predicted the school mean of teachers' internal accountability. The school mean of individualism (β=0.05, t(178)=3.355, p=.001), collectivism (β=0.07, t(178)=2.515, p=.001), and organizational support (β=0.07, t(178)=3.714, $p < .001$) were all positive significant predictors. The p-value of the interaction between the school mean of collectivism with the school mean of organizational support suggested a marginal negative relation (β=−0.03, t(178)=−1.822, p=.07). School size had no predictive effect, just like in predicting internal accountability at the individual level.

The amount of explained variance at the teacher level was 13% and at the school level was 53%. Similar to the model of external accountability, the total explained variance of the internal accountability model was 21%, meaning that this set of predictors also predicted about one-fifth of the variance between teachers' internal accountability scores.

Principals' accountability predicting teachers' accountability

In order to explore the predictive power of principals' accountability disposition for their teachers' accountability, we had to limit our teacher sample to that composed of the same six countries represented in the principal sample. To this reduced teacher sample, we added the principals' own accountability dispositions as predictors of teachers' accountability.

We first explored the relations between teachers and principals on both external and internal accountability. The correlation between teachers' external accountability score and the principals' external accountability score was significant ($r(1,894)=.167$, $p < .001$) but relatively small. We also found a significant correlation ($r(1,894)=.2219$, $p < .001$) between teachers' and principals' internal accountability, slightly larger than the correlation for external accountability. The significant correlations allowed the inclusion of principals' external and internal accountability in the models as school-level predictors. These models are shown in Table 4.35.

PRINCIPALS' EXTERNAL ACCOUNTABILITY AS A PREDICTOR OF TEACHERS' EXTERNAL ACCOUNTABILITY

The most striking finding is the predicting effect at the school level of principals' external accountability on teachers' external accountability ($\beta=0.07$, $t(109)=3.155$, $p=.002$). We found that at the individual level, teachers' collectivism ($\beta=0.11$, $t(1,879)=8.313$, $p < .001$) and organizational support ($\beta=0.15$, $t(1,879)=9.455$, $p < .001$) significantly predicted teachers' external accountability. Also, a positive marginal interaction between collectivism and organizational support was observed ($\beta=0.03$, $t(1,879)=1.690$, $p=.091$). All other variables failed to predict external accountability at the teacher level. At the school level, organizational support predicted teachers' external accountability ($\beta=0.11$, $t(109)=4.722$, $p < .001$), and school size was a positive marginal predictor ($\beta=0.02$, $t(109)=1.792$, $p=.075$).

Another notable finding is the 15% explained variance at the teacher level and 43% at the school level. Comparing the explained variance for the model without and with principals' external accountability as predictor in the six-country sample (see Appendix 3.5a, second part, columns M7 and M8), we saw no change at the teacher level and 8 percent points more explained variance at the school level (the level where the principal's score was added as a predictor). Considering the small change in other predictors, we may conclude that all extra variance was explained by principals' external accountability scores.

Table 4.35 Predictive Model for Teachers' External and Internal Accountability With Principals' External Respectively Internal Accountability as Predictor

	External Accountability		Internal Accountability	
	B(SE)	β	B(SE)	β
Fixed Part				
Intercept	3.94 (0.024)		4.51 (0.019)	
Gender	−0.03 (0.027)	−0.01	−0.04 (0.022)	−0.02†
Seniority	0.002 (0.001)	0.02	0.001 (0.001)	0.01
Individualism	0.01 (0.016)	0.01	0.04 (0.016)	0.03*
Collectivism	0.20 (0.024)	0.11***	0.22 (0.021)	0.12***
Org. Support	0.20 (0.021)	0.15***	0.08 (0.015)	0.06***
Org. Support x Individualism	0.004 (0.02)	0.003	−0.005 (0.021)	−0.003
Org. Support x Collectivism	0.06 (0.033)	0.03†	−0.03 (0.035)	−0.02
School size (Student Body/1000)	0.09 (0.049)	0.04†	0.02 (0.038)	0.004
School mean Individualism	0.04 (0.058)	0.01	0.16 (0.051)	0.06**
School mean Collectivism	0.025 (0.085)	0.005	0.26 (0.078)	0.06**
School mean Org. Support	0.30 (0.064)	0.11***	0.13 (0.052)	0.04*
School mean Individualism x School mean Org. Support	0.09 (0.145)	0.01	−0.02 (0.118)	−0.004
School mean Collectivism x School mean Org. Support	0.33 (0.226)	0.03	−0.06 (0.167)	−0.001
Principal External/ Internal Accountability	0.16 (0.051)	0.07**	0.22 (0.044)	0.07***
Random Part	*Variance*	*Explained Variance*	*Variance*	*Explained Variance*
$\sigma^2_{u_0}$	0.228	15%	0.164	14%
σ^2_e	0.031	43%	0.016	58%

Note: † $p < .1$, * $p < .05$, ** $p < .01$, *** $p < .001$; Gender: 0=Female, 1=Male.

PRINCIPALS' INTERNAL ACCOUNTABILITY AS A PREDICTOR
FOR TEACHERS' INTERNAL ACCOUNTABILITY

Similar to the relation between principals' and teachers' external accountability previously reported, within the model for teachers' internal accountability with principal's internal accountability disposition, at the school level principals' internal accountability significantly predicted teachers' internal accountability (β=0.07, $t(109)$=3.846, p < .001). We also included in this model, at the individual level, teachers' gender (β=−0.02, $t(1,879)$=−1.887, p=.059), individualism (β=0.03, $t(1,879)$=2.286, p=.022), collectivism (β=0.12, $t(1,879)$=10.511, p < .001), and organizational support (β=0.06, $t(1,879)$=4.941, p < .001), which significantly predicted teachers' internal accountability, though for gender only marginally. All other variables did not predict internal accountability at the teacher level. Again, collectivism and organizational support were the strongest predictors.

At the school level, next to principals' internal accountability, the school means of individualism (β=0.06, $t(109)$=3.656, p=.001), collectivism (β=0.06, $t(109)$=3.412, p=.001), and organizational support (β=0.05, $t(109)$=2.308, p=.023) significantly predicted teachers' internal accountability.

When looking at the explained variance, we see for principals' internal accountability a similar trend for the explained variance of the model as for external accountability. The amount of explained variance was at the teacher level 14% and 58% at the school level. The latter is in the six-country sample 20 percent points more than in the model without the principals' internal accountability included (see Appendix 3.5b, second part, columns M7 and M8). Thus, and similar to the case of external accountability, adding the principals' accountability made the predictive value of the models substantially stronger.

Prediction of teachers' accountability dispositions toward parents and school management

In order to examine differences between accountability audiences, we analyzed teachers' accountability dispositions toward parents and school management. As in the case of teachers' general external and internal accountability, hierarchical models were appropriate for the audience-focused accountability data.

Relationships between model variables

We first ran correlations to explore the relations between the teachers' external accountability dispositions toward parents and school management with cultural values (individualism and collectivism) and perceived organizational support (Table 4.36). We also included personal background variables (gender, seniority) and school size. As in the case for correlations between external and internal accountability and teacher variables, we see many

Table 4.36 Correlations Between Teacher Variables and Accountability Toward Parents and School Management

	Accountability Toward Parents	Accountability Toward Management
(1) Gender	−.017	−.045*
(2) Seniority	.040*	−.012
(3) External accountability	.464**	.543**
(4) Internal accountability	.331**	.475**
(5) Individualism	−.007	.054**
(6) Collectivism	.257**	.289**
(7) Organizational support	.152**	.314**
(8) School size	−.068**	−.078**

Note: * $p < .05$; ** $p < .01$; Gender: 0=Female, 1=Male.

significant correlations and thus the more advanced analyses of the relationships between the study variables with multilevel multiple linear regression models for predicting teachers' accountability toward parents and school management were appropriate.

In Table 4.37, we present the models for teachers' external accountability toward parents and school management. As we did earlier in regards to teachers' general external accountability, as a last step in the analysis, we included principals' own external accountability toward the respective audiences as a predictor for teachers' accountability toward these two audiences (Table 4.38).

In regard to accountability toward parents, calculation of the ICC showed that 12% of the total variance was located at the school level, where for accountability toward school management the variance at the school level was 25%. The amount of variance at the school level within the accountability model toward school management was surprisingly high.

Two more features of the models should be noted. When looking at the models, it appears that the variables used to predict general external accountability (see Table 4.34) are about equally successful in predicting the accountability dispositions toward the two audiences. Seniority predicted accountability toward parents but not toward school management. In other words, teachers who had more years of work experience in school tended to feel more accountable to parents than teachers with less work experience, but no difference was found for school management in this regard. At the school level, we see in both audience-specific accountability disposition models that the school mean of teachers' collectivism plays a role in predicting aggregated school accountability, which was not a predictor in the general external accountability model (see Table 4.34). Noteworthy, further,

Table 4.37 Prediction of Teachers' External Accountability Toward Parents and School Management

	Accountability Toward			
	Parents		School Management	
	B(SE)	β	B(SE)	β
Fixed Part				
Intercept	3.66 (0.028)		4.07 (0.03)	
Gender	0.01 (0.034)	0.003	−0.003 (0.023)	−0.001
Seniority	0.003 (0.002)	0.03*	0.001 (0.001)	0.01
Individualism	0.002 (0.025)	0.002	−0.01 (0.018)	−0.005
Collectivism	0.28 (0.034)	0.16***	0.25 (0.023)	0.14***
Org. support	0.12 (0.026)	0.09***	0.17 (0.022)	0.13***
Org. support x individualism	−0.02 (0.027)	0.02	0.004 (0.024)	0.002
Org. support x collectivism	0.03 (0.032)	−0.01	0.04 (0.028)	0.02
School size (size/1,000)	−0.003 (0.023)	−0.002	−0.001 (0.022)	−0.0004
School mean individualism	−0.15 (0.078)	−0.05†	0.11 (0.074)	0.04
School mean collectivism	0.61 (0.098)	0.16***	0.30 (0.130)	0.08*
School mean org. support	−0.05 (0.077)	−0.02	0.24 (0.079)	0.11**
School mean individualism x school mean org. support	−0.12 (0.184)	−0.02	0.12 (0.143)	0.02
School mean collectivism x school mean org. support	0.09 (0.131)	0.02	−0.07 (0.105)	−0.01
Random Part	*Variance*	*% Explained Variance*	*Variance*	*% Explained Variance*
$\sigma^2_{u_0}$	0.521	7%	0.307	11%
σ^2_e	0.061	23%	0.082	28%

Note: † $p < .1$, * $p < .05$, ** $p < .01$, *** $p < .001$; Gender: Female=0, Male=1.

is the absence of predictive value of the aggregated scores of organizational support at the school level within the model that predicts teachers' disposition toward parents. After these general observations, we now focus on the separate models for the two audiences.

Study findings 111

Table 4.38 Predictive Model for Teachers' External Accountability Toward Parents and School Management With Principals' Parents or School Management Accountability Scores as Predictors

	Toward Parents		Toward School Management	
	B(SE)	β	B(SE)	β
Fixed Part				
Intercept	3.63 (0.032)		4.08 (0.035)	
Gender	0.01 (0.041)	0.01	0.003 (0.029)	0.001
Seniority	0.003 (0.002)	0.03†	0.001 (0.001)	0.01
Individualism	0.01 (0.029)	0.005	−0.01 (0.02)	−0.004
Collectivism	0.26 (0.037)	0.14***	0.24 (0.025)	0.14***
Org. support	0.12 (0.029)	0.09***	0.15 (0.025)	0.11***
Org. support x individualism	−0.02 (0.033)	−0.01	−0.005 (0.027)	−0.004
Org. support x collectivism	0.005 (0.042)	0.003	0.03 (0.037)	0.02
School size (size/1,000)	−0.09 (0.063)	−0.04	0.1 (0.083)	0.05
School mean individualism	−0.22 (0.091)	−0.07*	0.14 (0.09)	0.04
School mean collectivism	0.45 (0.109)	0.10***	0.23 (0.153)	0.05
School mean org. support	−0.01 (0.095)	−0.004	0.18 (0.104)	0.07†
School mean individualism x school mean org. support	0.58 (0.273)	0.07*	0.44 (0.221)	0.05†
School mean collectivism x school mean org. support	−0.01 (0.395)	−0.001	0.02 (0.374)	0.002
Principal external accountability toward parents/ school management	0.11 (0.035)	0.08**	0.16 (0.046)	0.11**
Random Part	*Variance*	*Explained Variance*	*Variance*	*Explained Variance*
$\sigma^2_{u_0}$	0.531	6%	0.317	9%
σ^2_e	0.056	33%	0.078	29%

Note: † $p < .1$, * $p < .05$, ** $p < .01$, *** $p < .001$; Gender: 0=Female, 1=Male.

Teachers' external accountability toward parents

MODEL WITHOUT PRINCIPALS' ACCOUNTABILITY

At the first level, teachers' collectivism (β=0.16, t(2,540)=8.343, p < .001) and organizational support (β=0.09, t(2,540)=4,540, p < .001) were positive significant predictors of teachers' accountability disposition toward parents. The more teachers adhered to collectivistic views and the more they experienced organizational support, the higher their accountability disposition toward parents. Additionally, at the teacher level, teachers' seniority was a significant positive predictor of teachers' accountability disposition toward parents (β=0.03, t(2,540)=8.343, p=.045), meaning that the more work experience teachers had, the higher their accountability disposition toward parents. All other variables at the teacher level did not predict teachers' accountability toward parents. Of the two predictors at the teacher level, collectivism had a larger standardized coefficient than the regression coefficient for organizational support, meaning that collectivism had a slightly higher predictive value. There was no significant interaction effect between collectivism and organizational support, meaning that the regression coefficients for collectivism were similar for teachers across the whole range of organizational support. The second cultural value, individualism, as well as the interaction between individualism and organizational support, did not predict teachers' external accountability toward parents.

At the second level, school, the school mean of teachers' collectivism (β=0.16, t(178)=6.267, p < .001) positively predicted the school mean of teachers' accountability toward parents: the more teachers on average had collective feelings, the more they felt externally accountable toward parents (similar to the teacher level prediction by teacher collectivism). The school mean of teachers' organizational support was not a significant predictor of teachers' accountability toward parents at the school level, and the school mean of teachers' individualism was a marginally negative significant predictor (β=−0.05, t(178)=−1.895, p=.059). None of the interactions at the school level of the cultural values and organizational support were predictors of accountability toward parents. These results showed that the teachers' individualistic and collectivistic values predicted external accountability toward parents to a stronger degree than their background characteristics.

At the teacher level, the model explained 7% of the teacher variance and at the school level, it explained 23% of the school faculty variance. The total explained variance of the model is 9%, so about one-tenth of the variance between teachers in external accountability scores toward parents is explained by the cultural values and organizational support predictors together at the teacher and the school level.

CONTRIBUTION OF PRINCIPALS' EXTERNAL ACCOUNTABILITY TOWARD PARENTS TO TEACHERS' EXTERNAL ACCOUNTABILITY TOWARD PARENTS

In light of the findings in regard to differences between teachers' and principals' accountability dispositions toward parents (Table 4.15), we set out on an analysis to examine the contribution of principals' accountability disposition to the teachers' accountability toward parents in the same schools. In Table 4.38, we see that principals' external accountability predicted teachers' accountability toward parents.

Of the variance at the teacher level, 6% is explained and at the school level, 33%. Compared with the explained variance for the model without external accountability scores as predictors in the six-country sample (see Appendix 3.6a, second part, columns M7 and M8), we see almost no change at the teacher level, and 6 percent points rise in explained variance at the school level (the level of the included predictor). We may conclude that a high amount of extra variance was explained by adding principals' accountability toward parents in the model. The total model did explain a somewhat similar amount of variance (9.5%) as the model without the principals' scores included as predictor.

Teachers' external accountability toward school management

MODEL WITHOUT PRINCIPALS' ACCOUNTABILITY

Similar to the accountability model for accountability toward parents, both teachers' collectivism ($\beta=0.14$, $t(2,540)=10.557$, $p < .001$) and experienced organizational support ($\beta=0.13$, $t(2,540)=7.536$, $p < .001$) were positive significant predictors at the teacher level (see Table 4.38). The other cultural value, individualism, showed not to be a significant predictor, and no background predictors were found to predict teachers' external accountability toward school management. Similar to the external model, both interactions between school support and the cultural values were not significant predictors of teachers' accountability toward school management.

At the second (school) level, the school means of teachers' collectivism ($\beta=0.08$, $t(178)=2.282$, $p=.024$) and organizational support ($\beta=0.11$, $t(178)=3.008$, $p=.003$) were significant positive predictors for the school mean of teachers' external accountability toward school management. School size and the interactions between the school means of teachers' individualism and collectivism with the school mean of teachers' organizational support did not predict the school mean of teachers' accountability toward school management.

114 Study findings

The amount of explained variance at the teacher level was 11% and at the school level was 28%. The total explained variance of the model predicting teachers' external accountability toward school management was 15%, which is a bit more than in the model predicting teachers' accountability toward parents.

CONTRIBUTION OF PRINCIPALS' EXTERNAL ACCOUNTABILITY TOWARD
SCHOOL MANAGEMENT TO TEACHERS' EXTERNAL ACCOUNTABILITY
TOWARD SCHOOL MANAGEMENT

Similar to including principals' accountability disposition toward parents for predicting the teachers' accountability toward parents in the same schools, we included principals' accountability toward school management as a predictor for teachers' accountability toward school management (see Table 4.38). Principals' external accountability toward school management significantly predicted teachers' external accountability to this audience (β=0.11, t(109)=3.567, p=.001), as did teachers' collectivism and organizational support. At the second level, the prediction by contribution of organizational support to the model including principal contribution was marginally significant (β=0.07, t(109)=1.784, p=.077), as was the interaction of collectivism with organizational support (β=0.05, t(109)=1.978, p=.050).

Of the variance, 9% is explained at the teacher level and 29% at the school level. Compared with the explained variances for the model without principals' external accountability scores as predictor in the six-country sample (see Appendix 3.6b, second part, columns M7 and M8), we saw a small change at the teacher and again a large change at the school level, the level of the included predictor: a 12 percent point increase.

Prediction of principals' accountability dispositions

Relationships between model variables

In this section, we report on our findings on the prediction of principals' accountability dispositions by their cultural values and their organizational (board) support. We also included principals' background variables (gender and seniority) in the analytical model and school size as school characteristic. Table 4.39 shows the results of running correlations for the principal study variables: cultural values, accountability dispositions, and principals' and schools' background variables. The many significant correlations allowed for building predicting models.

Table 4.39 Correlations Between Principal Study Variables

	1	2	3	4	5	6	7
(1) Gender	–						
(2) Seniority	.053						
(3) External accountability	.007	.433**					
(4) Internal accountability	−.192*	−.035	−001				
(5) Individualism	−.125	.057	−.017	.646**			
(6) Collectivism	.187*	−.002	−.062	.105	.024		
(7) Organizational support	−.155	−.108	−.447**	.276**	.312**	−.201*	
(8) School size	−.036	−.045	−.317**	.284**	.217*	−.104	.655**

Note: * $p < .05$, ** $p < .01$; Gender: 0=Female, 1=Male.

Because of the small number of principals within schools and the small number of countries (six) where principal data were collected, hierarchical analysis like HLM was not possible (see Chapter 3 on the study methods for a more elaborated discussion). Therefore, a stepwise multiple regression model was developed for each of the accountability dispositions. First, we included principals' background variables and secondly the cultural values and organizational support. At the third step, similar to the teacher models, we included interactions between the cultural values and organizational support. Then, school size was added to the model. As a final step, we included dummy variables for each country in order to acquire insight into the possible predictive value of the principals' respective countries. We selected *Hungary* as a reference group since the country mean of *Hungary* was closest to the general sample means of the principals' accountability dispositions. Table 4.40 shows the models for predicting principals' external and internal accountability.

Prediction of principals' external accountability

Our regression analysis included two models: the first included background variables, cultural variables, and organizational support. In the second model, we added the country dummy variables. The significant predictors in the first model were principals' gender ($\beta=-0.20$, $t(123)=-2.44$, $p=.016$), individualism ($\beta=0.28$, $t(123)=3.30$, $p=.001$), collectivism ($\beta=0.34$, $t(123)=2.63$, $p=.010$), and the interaction between individualism and organizational support ($\beta=-0.19$, $t(123)=-2.30$, $p=.023$). In regard to the gender effect, the minus sign of the β implied that male principals felt less externally accountable than their female counterparts. Furthermore, the more

116 Study findings

Table 4.40 Regression Models for Predicting Principals' Accountability Without and With Dummy Variables for Countries

	External Accountability				Internal Accountability			
	Without Dummies		With Dummies		Without Dummies		With Dummies	
	B (SE)	β	B (SE)	β	B (SE)	β	B (SE)	β
(Constant)	2.67 (0.38)		2.70 (0.41)		3.34 (0.36)		3.27 (0.36)	
Seniority	0.01 (0.004)	0.13	0.01 (0.004)	0.12	0.01 (0.004)	0.14	0.005 (0.004)	0.12
Gender	−0.19 (0.08)	−0.20**	−0.09 (0.08)	−0.10	−0.07 (0.07)	−0.09	0.06 (0.07)	0.07
Individualism	0.14 (0.04)	0.28***	0.13 (0.04)	0.26***	0.06 (0.04)	0.14	0.05 (0.04)	0.10
Collectivism	0.21 (0.08)	0.34**	0.19 (0.08)	0.31*	0.26 (0.07)	0.48***	0.27 (0.07)	0.50***
Organizational support	0.09 (0.05)	0.18	0.07 (0.05)	0.14	0.02 (0.05)	0.03	−0.01 (0.05)	−0.03
Individualism x org. support	−0.10 (0.04)	−0.19*	−0.11 (0.04)	−0.22*	−0.02 (0.04)	−0.05	−0.03 (0.04)	−0.07
Collectivism x org. support	0.08 (0.05)	0.16	0.02 (0.05)	0.05	0.06 (0.05)	0.15	0.01 (0.04)	0.01
School size[a]	0.04 (0.07)	0.04	0.08 (0.09)	0.09	−0.08 (0.07)	−0.10	−0.08 (0.08)	−0.10
Being from Israel[b]			0.08 (0.12)	0.07			0.05 (0.11)	0.05
Being from the Netherlands			−0.42 (0.14)	−0.32***			−0.42 (0.12)	−0.36***
Being from South Africa			0.01 (0.15)	0.01			0.28 (0.13)	0.22*
Being from Spain			0.11 (0.22)	0.08			0.18 (0.19)	0.15
Being from Zimbabwe			0.15 (0.15)	0.12			0.18 (0.13)	0.15
R Square		0.18		0.29		0.11		0.32

Note: † $p < .1$, * $p < .05$, ** $p < .01$, *** $p < .001$; Gender: Female=0, Male=1; [a]Student body/1,000; [b] *Hungary* is used as reference group.

principals adhered to individualistic or collectivistic values, the higher their external accountability dispositions. The negative-sign interaction between individualism and organizational support indicated that the more principals adhered to individualistic views, the weaker the relation between principals' organizational support and their external accountability. All other variables did not predict principals' external accountability. Overall, the model without country dummy variables explained 18% of the variance of principals' external accountability scores.

When country dummy variables were included, the gender of principals lost its predictive value. Individualism (β=0.26, t(118)=2.92, p=.004), collectivism (β=0.31, t(118)=2.27, p=.025), and the interaction between individualism and organizational support (β=−0.22, t(118)=−2.67, p=.009) still predicted principals' external accountability in the same way as without dummy variables. Additionally, being from *the Netherlands* (β=−0.32, t(118)=−3.03, p=.003) had a negative influence on principals' external accountability score, meaning that *Dutch* principals were less externally accountable than principals from other countries. Most notable is the extra amount of variance explained when including the country dummies. The model including the country variables explained 29% of the variance in principals' external accountability score, 11 percent points more than without country dummies.

Prediction of principals' internal accountability

The number of variables that predicted principals' internal accountability was lower than in the model predicting principals' external accountability. Within the model without country dummy variables, only collectivism (β=0.48, t(123)=3.55, p=.001) significantly predicted principal internal accountability. In other words, the more principals maintain collectivistic views, the higher their internal accountability disposition. All other variables failed to predict principals' scores and the model explained 11% of the variance in the principals' internal accountability.

When country dummy variables were included, collectivism still predicted principals' internal accountability (β=0.50, t(118)=3.65, p < .001). Additionally, being a *Dutch* principal (β=−0.36, t(118)=−3.52, p=.001) and being a principal from *South Africa* (β=0.22, t(118)=2.14, p=.035) proved also to be significant predictors. The positive coefficient for *South African* principals meant that principals from *South Africa* scored higher on internal accountability. For principals from *the Netherlands*, the opposite was true: being *Dutch* resulted in a lower score for principals' internal accountability. Similar to the external accountability model, the predictive value of the internal accountability model was higher when country dummies were

118 *Study findings*

included: without these sets of variables, the explained variance was 11%, while with them explained variance rose to 32%. In both cases, this was due only to the scores of principals in a small number of countries.

Prediction of principals' accountability dispositions toward parents and school management

Relationships between model variables

We first ran correlations to explore the relations between the principals' accountability dispositions toward parents and school management with cultural values (individualism and collectivism) and perceived organizational support (Table 4.41). We also included personal background variables (gender, seniority) and school size. We concluded that the many significant correlations allowed for building predictive models similar to the models for external and internal accountability with stepwise regression. Again, we included as a last step the dummy variables for countries, with *Hungary* as the reference country. Table 4.42 shows the models for predicting principals' accountability toward parents and school management both with and without country dummies.

Prediction of principals' accountability toward parents

The significant predictors in the model for principals' accountability toward parents without country dummies were principals' gender ($\beta=-0.20$, $t(123)=-2.42$, $p=.017$), collectivism ($\beta=0.54$, $t(123)=4.20$, $p < .001$), and

Table 4.41 Correlations Between Principal Variables and Accountability Toward Parents and School Management

	Accountability	
	Toward Parents	Toward School Management
(1) Gender	−.224**	−.179*
(2) Seniority	.135	.019
(3) External accountability	.557**	.572**
(4) Internal accountability	.425**	−.499**
(5) Individualism	−.032	.009
(6) Collectivism	.135	.098
(7) Organizational support	.025	.090
(8) School size	−.072	−.145

Note: * $p < .05$, ** $p < .01$; Gender: 0=Female, 1=Male.

Table 4.42 Regression Models for Predicting Principals' Accountability Toward Parents and School Management Without and With Dummy Variables for Countries

	Accountability Toward Parents					Accountability Toward School Management				
	Without Country Dummies		With Country Dummies			Without Country Dummies		With Country Dummies	
	B (SE)	β	B (SE)	β		B (SE)	β	B (SE)	β
(Constant)	1.92 (0.55)		1.31 (0.59)			2.68 (0.56)		2.35 (0.60)	
Seniority	0.01 (0.006)	0.12	0.01 (0.006)	0.08		−0.002 (0.007)	−0.03	−0.003 (0.006)	−0.04
Gender	−0.29 (0.12)	−0.20*	−0.21 (0.12)	−0.15†		−0.25 (0.12)	−0.17*	−0.12 (0.12)	−0.09
Individualism	0.09 (0.07)	0.12	0.02 (0.07)	0.03		0.09 (0.07)	0.11	0.008 (0.07)	0.01
Collectivism	0.49 (0.12)	0.54***	0.63 (0.13)	0.69***		0.31 (0.12)	0.35*	0.39 (0.13)	0.43**
Organizational support	−0.08 (0.08)	−0.10	−0.02 (0.08)	−0.03		0.04 (0.08)	0.06	0.06 (0.08)	0.08
Individualism x org. support	−0.10 (0.06)	−0.13	−0.06 (0.06)	−0.08		−0.09 (0.06)	−0.11	−0.08 (0.06)	−0.11
Collectivism x org. support	0.32 (0.08)	0.44***	0.19 (0.05)	0.27**		0.31 (0.08)	0.44***	0.19 (0.08)	0.27*
School size[a]	−0.09 (0.11)	−0.07	0.10 (0.09)	0.08		−0.19 (0.11)	−0.14	0.02 (0.13)	0.12
Being from Israel[b]			−0.01 (0.18)	−0.003				0.23 (0.18)	0.14
Being from the Netherlands			−0.49 (0.21)	−0.25*				−0.58 (0.21)	−0.30**
Being from South Africa			−0.09 (0.22)	−0.04				0.001 (0.22)	0.001
Being from Spain			0.82 (0.33)	0.42*				0.65 (0.33)	0.33†
Being from Zimbabwe			−0.33 (0.22)	−0.16				−0.14 (0.23)	−0.07
R Square		0.24		0.36			0.19		0.33

Note: † $p < .1$, * $p < .05$, ** $p < .01$, *** $p < .001$; Gender: Female=0, Male=1; [a] Student body/1,000; [b] Hungary is used as reference group.

the interaction between collectivism and organizational support (β=0.44, $t(123)$=4.17, $p < .001$). Male principals felt less accountable toward parents than their female counterparts. The more principals adhered to collectivistic values, the higher their accountability toward parents. The interaction between collectivism and organizational support indicated that the more principals held to collectivistic views, the stronger the relationship between principals' organizational support and accountability toward parents. None of the other variables predicted principals' accountability toward parents. Overall, the model without country dummy variables explained 24% of the variance of principals' accountability toward parents.

When country dummy variables were included, the predictive value of gender of principals became marginally significant (β=−0.15, $t(118)$=−1.77, p=.079). Collectivism (β=0.69, $t(118)$=5.01, $p < .001$) and the interaction between collectivism and organizational support (β=0.27, $t(118)$=2.52, p=.013) still predicted principals' accountability toward parents in the same way as without dummy variables. Additionally, being from *the Netherlands* (β=−0.25, $t(118)$=−2.36, p=.020) had a negative influence on principals' external accountability score, meaning that *Dutch* principals were less accountable toward parents than principals from other countries. *Spanish* principals felt significantly more accountable toward parents than their colleagues in other countries (β=0.42, $t(118)$=2.48, p=.015). Most notable is the extra amount of variance explained when including the country dummies. The model including the country variables explained 36% of the variance in principals' accountability toward parents, 12 percent points more than in the model without country dummies.

Prediction of principals' accountability toward school management

In the model for principals' accountability toward school management without country dummies, we saw the same predictors and in the same direction as for accountability toward parents: principals' gender (β=−0.17, $t(123)$=−2.06, p=.041), collectivism (β=0.35, $t(123)$=2.60, p=.011), and the interaction between collectivism and organizational support (β=0.44, $t(123)$=3.97, $p < .001$). Male principals felt less accountable toward school management than their female counterparts. The more principals adhered to collectivistic values, the higher their accountability toward school management. The interaction between collectivism and organizational support indicated that the more principals adhered to collectivistic values, the stronger the relationship between principals' organizational support and their accountability toward school management. All other variables did not predict principals' accountability toward school management. Compared to the general external accountability model (Table 4.40) of the predictors, only collectivism had a similar role. Overall, the model without country dummy variables explained 19% of the variance of principals' accountability toward school management, a bit less than for accountability toward parents.

When country dummy variables were included, the predictive value of principals' gender disappeared. Collectivism (β=0.43, $t(118)$=3.04, p=.003) and the interaction between collectivism and organizational support (β=0.27, $t(118)$=2.45, p=.016) still predicted principals' accountability toward parents in the same way as without dummy variables.

Additionally, again, being from *the Netherlands* (β=−0.30, $t(118)$=−2.78, p=.006) had a negative influence on principals' external accountability score, whereas the positive relationship for *Spanish* principals was marginally significant (β=0.33 $t(118)$=1.94, p=.055). *Dutch* principals were less accountable toward school management than principals from other countries. Again, there was a considerable extra amount of variance explained when including the country dummies: 33% of the variance in principals' accountability toward school management, 14 percent points more than in the model without country dummies.

Prediction of accountability: summary

Teachers' accountability

The first notable finding on predicting teachers' external and internal accountability is the similarity of the signs of most significant coefficients. All coefficients had a positive sign, indicating that a higher score on one of these predictors increased teachers' accountability disposition. Organizational support and collectivism were the strongest predictors of teachers' accountability disposition at the teacher level. For external accountability, these were the only predictors at the teacher level. For internal accountability, other than individualism and collectivism, gender was a predictor as well (female teachers were more internally accountable). At the school level, the models differed from each other except for the school mean of collectivism that predicted both types of accountability. Internal accountability was also predicted by individualism and organizational support. In addition, principals' accountability proved to be a significant predictor of their respective school teachers' accountability: principals' external accountability predicted their teachers' external accountability, and principals' internal accountability predicted their teachers' internal accountability.

122 Study findings

In sum, in all eight countries, external and internal teachers' accountability were considerably related to the cultural values teachers held, more so with collectivism than with individualism. Organizational support was an even stronger predictor: the more teachers experienced support in their work, the more they felt both externally and internally accountable. Principals' external and internal accountability were also strong predictors of their respective teachers' external and internal accountability.

Teachers' accountability toward parents and school management

The first notable finding for accountability, specifically toward parents and school management, is the similarity of the predictors at the teacher level with those for predicting external accountability in general (for no specific audience). Within all three predictive models, teachers' collectivistic views and organizational support were important predictors of teachers' external accountability. Teachers' individualistic views failed to predict teachers' accountability scores in all three models (general, parents, and management). At the school level, more variations were found among the three predictive models. Most notable was the predictive value of the school means of teachers' collectivism in the models predicting accountability dispositions toward parents and school management, where this predictor failed to predict the teachers' general external accountability. Also notable was the failure of the school mean of teachers' organizational support to predict teachers' accountability dispositions toward parents. A final interesting finding is that the total amount of variance at the school level was substantively lower for the model predicting teachers' accountability dispositions toward parents (12%) than for the model predicting teachers' accountability dispositions toward school management (25%) and for general external accountability. Of the total variance, 19% was located at the school level.

Principals' accountability

Comparing the models that predicted teachers' external and internal accountability and the models that predicted principals' external and internal accountability, we see a similar trend. In all four models, the cultural values and organizational support played a predictive role, and both teachers' and principals' accountability disposition could be predicted to a reasonable degree. Female principals feeling a bit more externally accountable than their male colleagues is another feature of this model. The added explained variance in the model by including country dummy variables is striking, specifically that mainly one country, *the Netherlands*, is responsible for this effect.

Principals' accountability toward parents and school management

The models for predicting principals' accountability toward parents and school management follow the lines of the model for principals' external accountability, with collectivism and the interaction between collectivism and organizational support being the strongest predictors. Also, the gender effect and the added explained variance by the country dummies are noteworthy. Female principals feel somewhat more accountable toward parents and school management than do male principals.

Notes

1. The results of these tests are available from the authors on request.
2. Results for the Bonferroni post hoc test are available from the authors on request.

5 Discussion of study findings

Introduction

The previous chapter presented a wealth of findings on the study variables and the relationships among these variables. We described at length teachers' and principals' accountability dispositions, cultural values, and organizational support, all in relationship to each other and to background variables. The present chapter presents a discussion of the findings related to the core issues of the study. We start with discussing the differences in the two dimensions of accountability: external and internal. Special attention is paid to two accountability audiences: parents and school management. A unique issue is the predictive relation of principals' accountability to teachers' accountability. Then we move to the central topic of this book: the relations of cultural values – individualism and collectivism – to accountability on both personal and country levels. In the final section of this chapter, we focus on the role of organizational support in the research study model.

The two dimensions of accountability: external and internal

As described in the theoretical background to this book (Chapter 2), a two-way classification of accountability disposition was used in the present study: external and internal dimensions. The external dimension represents one's accountability disposition in relation to institutional rules and regulations. Accordingly, educators' external accountability refers to their inclination and willingness to comply with policy regulation and to report to their superiors. The internal accountability dimension, on the other hand, is more abstract, representing one's accountability in regard to inner professional and ethical standards, thus reporting to oneself. The basic rationale behind the two-way classification is recognition of employees' divided approaches when reacting to accountability expectations. Based on the relatively wide consensus among accountability researchers in regard to this dichotomy (Firestone & Shipps, 2005; Knapp & Feldman, 2012; Poulson, 1998), we have designed our study questionnaire to separately measure each of the two dimensions (see Chapter 3 – Study Methods, p. 29). Accordingly, one of the study challenges was to test whether the two measures reliably described the two discrete concepts. This challenge was approached through examination of the interrelations between the two, testing differences in scores on the two dimensions, and discerning the unique antecedents of each.

Interrelations between external and internal accountability dispositions

Correlation tests between the two accountability dimensions showed that in the case of principals, the interrelation was very close to zero (0.001); thus, the two dimensions were entirely different. In the case of teachers, though, the two dimensions correlated moderately (r=.50, $p < .01$), indicating that there was about a 25% shared explained variance between the two. We believe that the different results between the two groups – teachers and principals – may be explained by their different occupational status, as specified next.

Teaching is largely considered a semi-professional occupation, aspiring to become a full profession by complying with basic demands such as occupational-related knowledge and personal commitment (Krejsler, 2005) – two key characteristics of education. Both teachers and school principals (who are typically teachers by training and experience) are inherently committed to professional and ethical codes in their work, and thus are likely to be internally accountable. In the case of principals, professional responsibility is augmented by their status as instructional and team leaders (Hallinger et al., 2020) who are expected to define their school's mission, promote a positive learning climate, manage instructional programs, supervise teachers, advance empowerment among staff, perform administrative tasks, and more.

Both teachers and principals, as any employee in any working context, are expected to be externally accountable. In the case of teachers, this means reporting mainly to their immediate superior, the principal, and to parents, and other pedagogic coordinators, such as subject-area or age-level coordinators. For principals, external accountability is considerably more conspicuous than for teachers. Principals assume a heavy load of administrative and managerial duties *ex-officio*. Being restricted by high-stakes accountability policies such as the *No Child Left Behind Act* (2002) and *Every Student Succeeds Act* (2015) in the U.S., principals are accountable not only to audiences on the school grounds but also to external bodies like the local educational municipality or the national educational department. Accordingly, school performance and educational results strongly shape the success and careers of school principals. As heads of their schools' teaching faculties, principals' external accountability has still another unique aspect, in Lortie's words (2009): "The principalship is a particular kind of occupation: it is among those lines of work where one is held accountable for the performance of others who rank lower in the hierarchy" (p. 2). In short, external accountability in principals' work is strongly influenced by the administrative and managerial aspects of their work.

Differences among the nature of teachers' and principals' responsibilities may explain why only for principals no relation was found between internal and external accountability. For teachers, pedagogical and administrative duties are more or less harmoniously integrated in their class work, which explains the moderate correlation (where some of the explained variance was shared) found between the two accountability dimensions. Apparently, the shared variance between the two dimensions among teachers represented common fundamentals of both external and internal accountability in the same tasks: the willingness to report and be evaluated by clear standards (Frink & Ferris, 1998; Hall et al., 2007).

In the principals' case, however, the administrative work is largely managerial and somewhat separated from school-level pedagogical work. Principals' accountability is targeted not only to school stakeholders, where more internal accountability is expected, but also to bodies outside the school grounds, where external accountability is more likely to be anticipated. Hence, there is little correlation between external and internal accountability among principals in our study, unlike the case of teachers.

Internal accountability preferred over external accountability

The most striking finding of the mean comparison analyses between the two accountability dimensions was that the internal score was higher than that of the external: both teachers and principals reported being more internally than externally accountable. It is noteworthy that the significant difference between the two dimensions persisted across samples and in each and every country. A comparison between teachers' and principals' scores showed that principals were consistently higher than teachers on both external and internal accountability (external: M=4.19, M=3.90; and internal: M=4.58, M=4.47, respectively). The reason, perhaps, lies in the extra administrative (external) and instructional/professional leadership (internal) responsibility embedded in the managerial position compared to teachers' non-managerial roles. Also, the difference between teachers and principals was larger on external accountability than on internal accountability, which aligns with our previously stated reasoning about the different positions of the two groups.

These differences show that teachers and principals still put more emphasis on their inner professional principles than on external work aspects in their accountability approach. Pervasive efforts in many educational systems to promote teachers' and principals' external accountability, with measures such as value-added assessment (Amrein-Beardsley, 2019; Zamir, 2019), apparently have not been able to change this situation. The great emphasis placed by teachers and principals on internal accountability may be rooted in the motivational foundation of educators starting as early as the career-seeking stage. Results of the 2018 TALIS showed that the majority of the surveyed teachers (over 90%) mentioned that they chose the teaching profession because they wanted to contribute to the development of children and society (OECD, 2019) – an intrinsic rather than extrinsic motivation. In another study, students in teaching programs reported that they preferred intrinsic values (e.g., learning new things) over extrinsic ones (e.g., promotion, salary) (Pascual, 2009). The strong internal accountability disposition then reflects the typical, inherent, professional values of teaching and education.

Moreover, the consistent and across-the-board superiority of internal over external accountability can be explained in relation to the distinctive impact of the two types of accountability on one's work. External accountability is clearly more visible than internal accountability in daily school life. Performance indicators characterizing external accountability, such as students' evaluation reports and work assessments, are concrete and transparent to superiors, school faculty, parents, or the surrounding community in general. Internal accountability, on the other hand, consists of employees' inner performance standards and is not easily visible to the outside. Consequently, the existence of internal accountability may be unknown or at best only assumed. Even when these inner standards are applied to concrete performance, the transfer between the two spheres is not necessarily immediate, and the inner elements in performance results are not conclusive. These may be the reasons why teachers and principals more strongly stressed their commitment to internal accountability, so that their inner work-related motivation would be known, than to external accountability, where work results are easily accessible to the outside.

Alternatively, educators' motivation to emphasize their internal accountability may be related to a cognitive bias, such as the social desirability effect. This phenomenon, widely documented in social research, describes a response set where respondents tend to falsify responses in order to conform to social expectations, similarly to some degree to the impression management phenomenon (Larson, 2019; Lavrakas, 2008). The result of this effect is that respondents' behavior may not consist of their pure, actual opinions but of deception and the transfer of their original opinion to one that is perceived publicly as more acceptable (Leng et al., 2020). In education, Khanolainen (2019) reported that teachers' attitudes toward new standards in a Russian school district were affected by a social desirability bias. In this case, because of disenchantment from school and government accountability systems, educators reacted by developing attitudes and behavior that seemed to them more socially desirable. Thus, the possibility of reporting higher internal than external accountability because of social desirability bias should be taken into account. In light of the strong preference showed by teachers and principals toward internal accountability, the possibility of social desirability bias in educators' work reports should be considered.

Accountability audiences: parents and school management

In this section, we discuss teachers' and parents' external accountability to parents and school management. We focus on the former audience because external accountability toward management is essentially a default, while parents' status as a legitimate audience is often controversial. We start with a discussion of the role of the audience in reflecting the situational aspect of accountability.

Accountability audiences as a situational aspect of accountability

While personal accountability is perceived in this study primarily as an individual disposition, we have explored the question of whether accountability perception can be at the same time situational, namely whether it varies across contexts. We have focused our attention in this regard on two key audiences in educational accountability: parents and school management. Our question regarding the situational view of external accountability was addressed in the following two ways. First, the scale used to measure audience-related accountability was a shorter form of the original external accountability measure employed for the all-country analyses (see Chapter 3 – Study Methods, p. 29). The items taken from the original scale were modified to specifically target the respective audience. Results showed that correlations between the general external accountability score and the two audience-related external accountability scores of teachers and principals were moderate (r=.446 to .572; see Table 4.12). These results indicated that the dispositional scores were not perfectly constant for either teachers or principals across situations; in other words, the targeted audience made a difference in the accountability disposition.

Second, tests of correlation performed between accountability to parents and accountability to school management among the two study samples – teachers and principals – disclosed another situational effect. The correlation pertaining to principals was considerably higher than that of parents (r=.762, r=.452, respectively; see Table 4.12), namely external accountabilities to parents and to management were more similar to one another among principals than teachers. This difference indicates that situational effects may rest also with the accountability agents (principals and teachers in this case).

While each of the previous findings by itself is insufficient to conclude that situational characteristics influence accountability dispositions, the overall picture leads to a consistent conclusion – that audience matters in assessing accountability. Although perceived accountability is defined in our study (see Chapter 2 – Teachers' and Principals' Accountability: Theoretical Background, p. 6–8) as an individual disposition, it still may vary according to a situational context such as audience or agent status. This argument is in accordance with Davis-Blake and Pfeffer (1989), who showed that job attitudes reflecting personal dispositions are also related to situational factors. In the present study, the audience-centered situational condition consists of teachers' and principals' differential interactions with school parents and superiors. Future studies ought to test this assertion on work interactions pertaining to additional school stakeholders (for example, students and teacher-colleagues).

Differences in accountability to parents versus school management

It seems that the most conspicuous finding in regard to audience-focused external accountability was the difference between accountability disposition to parents and school management. Results showed that both teachers and principals tended to feel substantially and significantly more accountable toward their superiors (school management or school board, respectively) than to parents. This higher accountability toward management than parents repeated across the board for each separate country in both teacher and principal samples. Though astonishing, these results are generally consistent with common practices of school operations and literature on parental involvement.

These results reflect the fact that school operations inherently involve a regulatory policy of mandatory teacher reports to school management, followed by principal feedback and possibly appropriate administrative action.

Similarly, principals would typically report to their respective educational boards, followed by feedback and possibly administrative action. Other than the formal aspect of these work relations, external accountability also means that teachers and principals would be inherently inclined to report on their work outcomes as part of their professional inner inclination, which is the subjective counterpart of external accountability, a core concept of the present study.

The results pointing at the significantly and substantially lower teacher accountability to parents than to school management warrant special attention. The unique status of school parents may provide an explanation. Although undeniably a relevant and entitled audience, parents' status in schools is vague and sometimes controversial. Teachers often tend to view parents as interfering somewhat with teachers' professional work (Hornby & Lafaele, 2011). Therefore, teachers may not see relations with parents as a necessary part of their professional responsibilities (Egger et al., 2015). Added to the largely informal nature of teachers' reporting to parents, it is clear why external accountability to parents was lower than that to school management.

As mentioned earlier, principals' accountability to parents was significantly higher than that of teachers. This finding may be attributed to the different type of relationship each of the two groups has with parents. Principals typically deal with parent organizations (school, district, or national level) more than with single parents. Although principal-parent relations may potentially be conflictual (Lareau & Muñoz, 2012), when dealing with organized parent groups, legitimacy probably prevails. Principals' relations with parent organizations would typically deal with matters related to school operations, where parents voice their opinions and offer their input. Principals, therefore, may view parental involvement as supportive of their managerial work, similarly to their view of school boards, to which they are formally accountable. This assertion is consistent with the higher correlation mentioned previously between accountability to parents and the school board for principals. Both audiences may be perceived by principals as essential school resources.

In contrast to accountability to parents, as described previously, no significant difference was found between teachers and principals in regard to school management. Similarly, no such difference was found in any of the separate countries. This may be explained by the formal status of a school as well as board management. Although accountability in the present study is defined as a subjective term, accountability to management is mandatory after all; thus, the motivation to comply is less flexible than the motivation to be accountable to parents, hence the little difference between principals and teachers in regard to management.

Effect of principals' accountability on teachers' accountability

We were interested in the contribution of principals' own accountability to teachers' accountability in general and in regard to each of the two specific audiences: parents and school management. Our question was: does the principal's personal accountability catalyze teachers' personal accountability? This question was triggered by studies on a spillover effect of managerial attitudes on subordinates' attitudes (e.g., Coget, 2011). Results (Table 4.35, 4.38) in the present study showed that the higher the principals' sense of external and internal accountability was, the more their respective teachers said they were accountable in the respective accountability dimensions. This effect repeated consistently in each of the specific audiences studied (parents and school management) as well as when the audience was not specifically mentioned. Apparently, school leadership was influential in motivating teachers to express accountability by setting an example of being accountable themselves.

These results are in line with the Leader-Member Exchange (LMX) Theory applied to relations between school principals and teachers. Somech and Wenderow (2006), for instance, showed that the directive leadership style predicted teachers' performance. In another application of this theory to school context, Zeinabadi (2014) found that principals are instrumental in motivating teachers to trust in leaders and become 'organizational citizens' when their principals are perceived as practicing procedural justice. Based on these studies, as well on the present study findings, we recommend that more rigorous research be designed to identify potential mediating and moderating factors that may explain these relations. It is possible, for example, that the spillover effect of principals' accountability to teachers' accountability will be stronger in participative rather than directive school cultures because participative management would create an atmosphere of trust in the leader. Finally, our results mean that focusing on increasing principals' sense of accountability could lead not only to results at the school leadership level but also at the respective faculty level.

Predicting accountability by personal individualism and collectivism

A major objective of the present study was to examine the prediction effect of two cultural values, individualism and collectivism, on teachers' and principals' accountability dispositions. The wealth of theoretical and empirical literature on these values (e.g., Gelfand et al., 2007; House et al., 2004; Kim, 1995; Triandis, 1995), as well as the nature of our multi-country study sample, enabled the use of two settings in explaining the relations of the cultural values to accountability: one venue, described in this section, is focused on personal-level values, and the other on country-level values, as described in the next section.

Relations of individualistic and collectivistic personal values to accountability

Results showed that collectivism, more than individualism, was a leading characteristic of teachers' and principals' cultural-values makeup. Teachers and principals alike tended to score significantly higher on collectivism than individualism and the effect size was quite high – nearly one Cohen's d (Tables 4.17 and 4.18, respectively). The relationship of teachers' and principals' individualism to accountability was weaker, if present at all, and different between the two groups.

The vital role of collectivism (compared to individualism) in teachers' and principals' work life should be viewed in comparison with the unique institutional characteristics of schools. Although teachers may work in their classrooms rather independently, overall educational work is by nature a collective endeavor for the well-being and development of youth. To achieve the best possible educational results for students, a concerted effort by all parties involved (e.g., subject-specific teachers, class-area and subject-area coordinators, homeroom teachers, pedagogical coordinators, parents) is needed. This complex project requires the highly collaborative work of all school stakeholders. Participants in such joint efforts are likely to succeed in their educational mission if they perform in a community-oriented environment that supports collectivist values. When adhering to collectivist values in an educational institution, these participants feel responsible for the well-being and learning of students and ready to be accountable for that to the larger community.

This community approach to schools has been supported by scholars such as Furman (2002), who viewed the school community as based on belonging and relationships, namely, a collectivistic ground. From a philosophical perspective, Starrat (2007) conceptualized the school community as centering on professional ethics and morality. A more applied approach was taken by Smetackova et al. (2020) in a recent multi-country study. These authors showed specifically that core principles of the school community idea improved a wide range of school missions: education, communication and a positive climate for students, collaboration of the school with the surrounding community, and sharing values and vision. Consistent with this school-as-community approach, teachers in the present study apparently tended to align their perceived accountability dispositions more with the context of being members of a collective (the school faculty) than with being independent individuals. Similarly, principals probably targeted their accountability tendencies more toward their respective school community as a whole rather than toward their own individual aspirations.

The community approach to schools may help to resolve what looks like an inconsistency between our study results and arguments of authors such as Gelfand et al. (2004) regarding the links between personal accountability and the two values of individualism and collectivism. These authors claimed that, in collectivistic cultures, people were expected to share responsibility with their community members, and therefore their accountability rested with the group. In individualistic cultures, on the other hand, where people tended to take personal responsibility for their own actions, accountability rested primarily with the individual to a larger degree than in collectivist cultures. Individualistic employees, then, were likely to feel more highly accountable than their collectivist counterparts. Similarly, Velayutham and Perera (2004) who studied general (non-educational) organizations, claimed that, in collectivistic societies, accountability would be lower than in individualistic ones, the reason being that shame, a typical characteristic of collectivist societies, would prevent employees from reporting fully and transparently on failing work results.

These suppositions seem to be in contrast with the present study's results, where collectivism predicted accountability to a larger degree than individualism across the board. We suggest that the unique school work context played a role in the way cultural values were related to personal accountability. Because school was often perceived as a professional community, collectivistic values of both teachers and principals were stronger than individualistic values, reinforced by collegial and emotional ties with school members, to influence educators' accountability.

Prediction of accountability by personal individualism and collectivism

Our prediction analyses (HLM in the case of teachers and multivariate regression for principals) showed that collectivism was a much stronger predictor of accountability than individualism. The more teachers and principals adhered to collectivistic values, the more they felt externally and internally accountable. Individualism predicted internal accountability among teachers (at both individual and school levels), while among principals it predicted external accountability. These opposing findings are very likely to be rooted in the different work contexts of the two types of educators.

Teachers are natural members of the school faculty, where the core mission is to benefit the school's students through the best teaching and ethical practices. It seems that internal accountability, in contrast to its external

134 Discussion of study findings

counterpart, was associated in the case of teachers with values represented by individualism – the need to achieve and be a better teacher through emphasis on professional and ethical standards. As members of professional school communities, teachers' individualistic values in the present study unsurprisingly tended to relate to internal accountability, which is inherently focused on professional and ethical codes of conduct, more than to external accountability.

The relation of principals' individualism to external accountability seems also to be rooted in the formal and contextual circumstances of their work, but in a different way. Similar to teachers, principals are also part of a professional school community. However, unlike teachers, principals are positioned at the top of the school's administrative hierarchy and are often individually held accountable in regard to school success. In a different study conducted among principals in six countries and focused on work responsibilities, a considerable proportion of responsibilities as perceived by the principals themselves were management-related, such as administrative style, administrative duties, personnel management, and student affairs management (Chan et al., 2019). Given the wide range of managerial responsibilities, individualistic principals may be driven more toward external than internal accountability because complying with institutional policy and regulation is perceived as critical for recognition and promotion. This is probably the reason for the link between individualism and external accountability for principals in the present study.

Finally, these differential results of the cultural values vis-à-vis accountability dimensions contribute to the theoretical distinction between external and internal accountability, as originally conceived by a number of authors (Firestone & Shipps, 2005; Knapp & Feldman, 2012; Poulson, 1998), and adopted in this study. Our findings showed that each dimension can be characterized by different antecedents.

Prediction of accountability to parents and school management by personal individualism and collectivism

Our main purpose in the study of accountability audiences was to compare between the predictive value of teachers' cultural values to parents and school management. For that purpose, we applied the same model used in our study for general external accountability (see Chapter 4 – Study Findings, p. 108). As recalled, the hierarchical model included two levels of analysis: the individual teacher level and the aggregated teacher group (teacher faculty) level. At the individual level, results were similar to those found for general external accountability, but with a lower predictive value: teacher collectivism and school support predicted accountability to both parents and school management. On top of that, individualism had no predictive effect. Different results were found for collectivism at the teacher faculty level: while in the general accountability model faculty collectivism had no predictive effect, here faculty collectivism significantly predicted accountability to parents and, to a lesser degree, to school management. Apparently, as a group, teachers tend to see school as a community, where members share common values, support, and mutual accountability (Weathers, 2011). The more teachers see all stakeholders (particularly parents) as part of the school community, and the higher their collectivism sense, the higher the external accountability to the two audiences. It is likely that being part of a professional group (teacher faculty) contributes to an increased collective identity and a higher tendency to be accountable to the various community members. It should be noted that between the two levels of analysis, the group (teacher faculty) level explained the bulk of the accountability variance. Thus, looking at the group, not only at individual teachers, considerably contributes to our ability to understand and predict external accountability to parents and school management.

Accountability at a country level

This study is based on the premise that the cultural values to which people adhere are key variables that may help explain the level of teachers' and principals' accountability disposition. The previous section focused on *personal* cultural values as predictors of accountability. Here, we look at *country* cultural values as predictors. The country, then, is regarded as an overarching cultural entity, representing the aggregate scores of its respective respondents. In the present section, we discuss our findings regarding country value effects on accountability.

Country similarities and differences in accountability

Generally, countries' scores on external and internal accountability were relatively high (mean 3.90 and 4.47, respectively, for teachers; 4.19 and 4.75, respectively, for principals, on a 1–5 scale; Table 4.1). Analysis of difference was performed in order to detect which countries were similar or different from each other. In regard to *teachers*, clustering analysis of countries' accountability means showed significant differences. *South Africa, Israel,* and *Zimbabwe* had significantly higher scores than all other countries on external accountability, whereas *Canada, Spain, China,* and *the Netherlands* were lowest. On internal accountability, *South Africa, Israel,*

Canada, and *Hungary* were highest among teachers, whereas *the Netherlands* stood alone with the lowest score. As for principals, *South Africa*, *Israel*, and *Zimbabwe* were highest on external accountability, whereas *the Netherlands*, *Spain*, and *Hungary* were lowest. The *Dutch principals'* score was significantly lower than all other five countries on internal accountability. We will come back to this last finding in the next section.

Putting it all together, in our sample *South Africa* and *Israel* stand out as relatively high-accountability countries in the two accountability dimensions as well as in both samples – teachers and principals. *Zimbabwe* also has high scores in the principals' sample. *The Netherlands* emerges as the lowest in both dimensions and both samples compared to all other countries. Reasons for similarity among *South Africa*, *Israel*, and *Zimbabwe* could lie in all three countries having education departments that are highly bureaucratic. In *South Africa* and *Zimbabwe*, the current governments inherited bureaucratic systems from the former white respective colonial regimes and tended to hold control through tight governmental regulation including, for example, rigid regulations regarding professional development that perhaps contributed to enhanced teachers' internal accountability (Booyse, 2015; Mpungose & Ngwenya, 2017). In *South Africa*, the government explicitly and forcefully implemented accountability measures (Chidozie, 2017), perhaps affecting teachers' compliance with high external accountability. In *Israel*, governmental regulation in education has been high traditionally, mostly for political and ideological reasons (Berkovich, 2019; Gibton, 2011). When the presence of such a tightly controlling and monitoring government system are likely to lead to teachers' and principals' enhanced accountability, one may expect *China* to similarly show high accountability scores. Indeed, *China*'s relatively low teacher accountability scores were striking. It may reflect the response of Chinese educators to low perceived organizational support in the Chinese educational system (see later in the present chapter). The Chinese low accountability scores may be also explained by the political system and culture, where strong emphasis on hierarchy (Rasmussen & Zou, 2014) may hinder teachers' feelings of personal accountability.

Differences in teachers' and principals' accountability dispositions may result from the context of the surrounding accountability system, in particular its structure and ideology. Two multi-country studies focused on the effect of national accountability systems on teachers and school leaders. Müller and Hernández (2010), in a study in seven European countries, investigated teachers' responses to national configurations of accountability policy. Although they found as a common trend that teachers distrusted most forms of accountability, they also saw differences between countries.

Discussion of study findings 137

In fact, educational policy regarding state-initiated standardization and accountability measures varied greatly within these seven countries. Following Darling-Hammond and Ascher (1991), they identified bureaucratic-, managerial-, and professional-accountability forms. Whereas, for example, in some countries accountability configurations emphasized the professional character of teaching, other systems focused on a simplistic managerial, performance-oriented form of accountability. In the context of professional accountability, moral commitments toward pupils' well-being and their care lay at the core as opposed to academic performance, high-stakes testing, and public ranking of schools in a managerial approach. Teachers' experiences of accountability varied with these policy approaches, with a more positive stance toward accountability in professional-oriented policies than in managerial and bureaucratic policies.

In a study on school leaders, Easley and Tulowitzki (2016) explored the effect of accountability policy in 12 countries. They investigated the way the philosophical underpinning of such policy defined accountability in each country, and how analysis of accountability policy can inform possibilities for educational improvement. In four of these countries (Australia, New Zealand, the U.S., and Chile), they observed that accountability standards and mechanisms varied widely both between and within countries. Educational infrastructures in these countries also played a critical role in the way principals were able to achieve their goals. The different standards and physical conditions occupied a problematic position in principals' work concerning the expectations of various school stakeholders. In three Asian countries – China, Hong Kong, and India – these researchers observed that when external accountability measures dominated internal ones, teachers were continuously criticized, resulting in teacher burnout. Finally, a review of five European countries – Austria, Germany, France, the Netherlands, and Norway – showed "a national and cultural touch" in the form of accountability demands on school governance. These 12 country accounts, other than pointing at differences and commonalities among countries, showed that school accountability posed a huge challenge for principals. The interplay between internal and external accountability, the adopted governing mechanisms, and the need to ensure the cooperation of various school stakeholders took a considerable toll on school administrators.

Both studies described previously (Easley & Tulowitzki, 2016; Müller & Hernández, 2010) inform us of the significant role of country accountability structure on teachers' and principals' attitudes and behavior at work. Our present study continues this line by focusing on the way country characteristics affect teachers' and principals' perceived sense of accountability.

Country similarities and differences in cultural values

Country-specific analyses showed that among teachers, collectivism outweighed individualism in each country with no exceptions (see Tables 4.17 and 4.18). Among principals, collectivism was also significantly higher than individualism in all countries except for *Spain*, where the opposite was true: *Spanish* principals adhered more to individualistic than to collectivistic values. On both measures, the *Spanish* principals had extreme scores compared to their colleagues in other countries. They had the highest on individualism and the lowest on collectivism. We will come back to this later.

Country means on each of the two cultural values varied considerably. Among teachers, collectivism scores ranged from *China* (lowest) to *Spain* (highest). As for individualism, *South Africa* was the lowest and *Zimbabwe* was the highest. Among principals, collectivism scores varied between *Spain* (lowest) and *Zimbabwe* (highest), while on individualism exactly the opposite order was true: *Zimbabwe* was the lowest and *Spain* was the highest. The order of collectivism scores for principals and teachers did not always align. For example, *Spanish* teachers had the highest score on collectivism whereas principals had the lowest.

The results for *Spain* clearly deserve special attention. *Spanish* principals had the highest score on individualism and the lowest on collectivism, which is an anomaly and may be a result of their need for support for doing their job and their feeling of a lack of autonomy, as inferred from the TALIS 2018 results (OECD, 2019). The TALIS 2018 study compared, among many other things, principals' job features in 48 countries, including five from our study: *Hungary*, *Israel*, *the Netherlands*, *South Africa*, and *Spain*. Results showed that principals in *Spain*, more than in most other countries, felt a need for support and reported having no say on important aspects of their work. Similarly, our own results (see Figure 4.9) showed an extremely low score of *Spanish* principals for perceived organizational support. By not feeling supported, their adherence to the group aims and values was possibly hurt. So, apparently *Spanish* principals felt, more than their colleagues in other countries, a lack of autonomy that may have made them adhere less to collectivistic and more to individualistic values. *Spanish* principals' lowest scores on collectivism perhaps highlighted a tension in the *Spanish* culture where more organizational support might be expected by principals and teachers than what was really offered. Such an expectation, which may be an indication of collectivist values, is met for teachers by their principal's support. However, principals feel slighted when they perceive little or no organizational support provided, and, consequently, their sense of belonging to an educational community is damaged, which may be expressed through their reporting less collectivism.

Discussion of study findings 139

As mentioned in the theoretical chapter (Chapter 2), we compared the study teacher and principal scores with the GLOBE in-group collectivism scores for the respective countries (see Figure 5.1). No clear similarity or difference between the study collectivism and the GLOBE in-group collectivism scores emerged. The correlations between the GLOBE scores and the teachers' and principals' collectivism scores were not significant and were weak: 0.07 for teachers and for principals even negative, −0.17. *Dutch* teachers and principals had low collectivism scores both in our study and in the GLOBE study.

In conclusion, except for *the Netherlands*, the collectivism scores in our sample are not clearly consistent with the in-group collectivism scores in the GLOBE project. This incompatibility between the two measures, in spite of the similar collectivism scales for the same countries, may be explained by the different samples in the two studies. While the GLOBE project respondents included managers from a large spectrum of organizations, our study was conducted exclusively on school teachers and principals. The difference between general managers and teachers can be explained by the different status of each group. The difference between general managers and school principals may be explained by the school organizational culture. As specified previously, schools are characterized by a unique culture of professional communities, where different stakeholders, such as teachers,

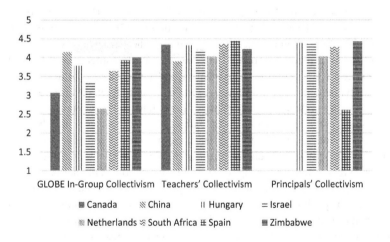

Figure 5.1 Teachers' and Principals' Collectivism per Country in This Study and In-Group Collectivism Scores (Practice) From the GLOBE Project (Rescaled to Run From 1–5); Retrieved on March 29th (14.50–14.58), 2020 From https://globeproject.com/results?page_id=country#list

students, and parents, form cohesive collectives. Principals' collectivism then is likely to target these school communities, whereas general managers would focus on other sets of collectives.

Country effect on accountability

This sub-section approaches the associations found between accountability and cultural values in two ways. First, we discuss the variance in accountability scores explained by the country factor. Second, we examine teachers' and principals' accountability dispositions in light of the countries' in-group collectivism. Finally, we look at principals' country affiliation as a predictor of their accountability dispositions.

Results on accountability scores in different countries revealed that teachers' external and internal accountability scores were related to country affiliation for about 12% of the variance (see Chapter 4 – Study Findings, p. 78). For the principals, country affiliation was even related to 19% of the variance in their external accountability and 28% of the variance in their internal accountability (Chapter 4, p. 79). These results are based on the multivariate analyses of variance that do not account for the variance explained by other variables that might overlap with the country. Thus, these analyses provide an estimation of the maximum variance related to teachers' and principals' country. For the principals, we also have an indication of the influence of country affiliation on accountability dispositions from the predictive models. Here, we see that for external accountability about 10% and for internal about 20% of the variance is related to country affiliation (Chapter 4, p. 117–118). For accountability toward parents, the percentage was similar and for school management a little bit lower, 14% (Chapter 4, p. 120–121). As expected, based on the large within-country variance in cultural values, the individual collectivism scores are more strongly related to accountability dispositions than the relationship of the country with accountability.

These percentages of explained variance show that accountability dispositions, both external and internal, were not only a consequence of the individuals' unique makeup but also a product of a society's or country's essence that collectively inspired its country's people. This national inspiration apparently affected teachers and principals above and beyond their personal dispositions. The nature of this national effect has not directly been investigated in the present study. However, when looking at the in-group collectivism score as measured in the GLOBE project (see Figure 5.2), there seems to be a slight tendency that the higher a country's in-group collectivism, the higher were the accountability dispositions in our study. The correlations between in-group collectivism and teachers' and principals' external and internal accountability (see Table 5.1) are all positive and have rather strong effect sizes. This is in line with the fact that teachers'

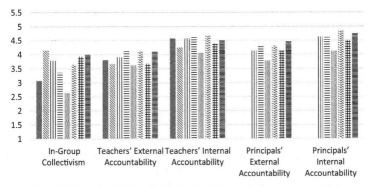

Figure 5.2 Teachers' and Principals' External and Internal Accountability per Country in This Study and In-Group Collectivism Scores (Practice) From the GLOBE Project

Table 5.1 Correlations of Teachers' and Principals' External and Internal Accountability Dispositions and Countries' In-Group Collectivism From the GLOBE Project

Teachers' Accountability		Principals' Accountability	
External	Internal	External	Internal
0.20	0.25	0.75*	0.75*

Note: * $p < .05$.

and principals' collectivism were strong predictors of their accountability dispositions. The correlations are higher for principals than teachers and only significant for principals. Of course, we should be cautious in interpreting the non-significant teachers' correlations, but because of the very small number of observations (eight countries for teachers) we also do not want to ignore these.

In addition to using country differences in accountability scores and countries' in-group collectivism as indicators for accountability scores, we used principals' country affiliation as a predictor of their external and internal accountability dispositions (Table 4.40). As recalled, for teachers it was impossible to use country affiliation as a predictor because of the HLM analyses that did not allow the inclusion of a small number of countries (Chapter 3 – Study Methods, p. 32). Only *the Netherlands* came up as a predictor in the principal analyses, negatively affecting principals' accountability: the higher the likelihood of being affiliated with *the Netherlands*, the higher were both accountability dimensions. This result is in line with the low accountability scores of *Dutch* principals and teachers mentioned previously. Because *the Netherlands* is so different from other countries, we will expand on explaining these results.

The relatively low external accountability of teachers and principals in *the Netherlands* may be connected to the constitutional freedom of education in that country. Article 23 of the constitution reads: "Providing education is free, taking into account the government's supervision of education and the government's care for the competence and morality of teachers." The government's responsibility for the level of education materializes primarily in setting the standards for national matriculation exams. It is the right and responsibility of the schools to define the curriculum that will help students to reach the nationally set aims. A topic of continuous debate is if the national inspectorate is allowed to supervise the way schools implement their curriculum. In any case, teachers and schools have considerable freedom in how they teach. In such a system, one could understand that the teachers and principals feel externally accountable when it comes to the matriculation results but that in other aspects they feel rather free.

A second reason for an overall lower accountability disposition (both internally and externally) of teachers in *the Netherlands* might be the fact that *the Netherlands* stands out in the proportion of teachers who have part-time jobs. In *the Netherlands*, the proportion of part-time teachers (50.5%) is twice as high as in the countries of the Organization for Economic Cooperation and Development on average (24.6%) (OECD, 2003). It is not far-fetched to assume that part-time teachers feel less accountable than full-time teachers because they can only influence their students for part of the day.

Finally, it is interesting to mention that for principals in *the Netherlands* we found a negative relation between their experience and external accountability, and this might have a relationship with the generally relatively low principals' external accountability. *The Netherlands* has a history of many government-initiated educational innovations (see Wubbels & van Tartwijk, 2018). Wubbels and van Tartwijk argue that *Dutch* educational professionals may have become tired of having to introduce innovations again and again. Also, the inspectorate is quite intrusive in monitoring schools that do not do well in student outcomes (Ehren & Shackleton, 2016), making principals focus mainly on student outcomes and having less interest in other accountability topics. We should, however, emphasize that although *Dutch* scores are lower than in other countries, they are still high enough to conclude that *Dutch* principals also feel considerably accountable.

Individualism and collectivism on both personal and country levels: continuum or mutual exclusiveness

To conclude the sections on cultural values, we turn back to the debate on whether individualism and collectivism should be considered to be opposite ends of a pole representing one dimension or two different concepts (Triandis, 1993). Our results did not provide any decisive answer. For example, *South Africa* teachers' scores indicated that the two were opposites of one dimension: scores were lowest on individualism and second highest on collectivism. However, *China*'s scores point in the direction of two mutually exclusive concepts: *China* was both low on collectivism (lowest) and on individualism (third lowest). *The Netherlands* was second highest on collectivism but also second highest on individualism. So, our results give no final answer pro or contra the existence of one or two dimensions. It is possible, though, that the meanings of individualism and collectivism are not exactly the same in each country and that they are interpreted differently in each culture. Thus, while in *South Africa* collectivism means, among other things, to be attentive to group interests and at the same time not to self-interests, in *China* and *the Netherlands* principals and teachers may be highly collectivistic in their concern about colleagues and at the same time also be highly individualistic in regard to their own personal aspirations. These interpretations are of course speculative and future research has to be conducted, presumably with qualitative studies, to understand interrelationships among cultural values. As specified in the Theoretical Background chapter (Chapter 2, p. 18), our study is based on the mutually exclusive assumption, although the differences found among countries in the cultural values interrelations should give us some concern as to the interpretations of our results.

Organizational support as a predictor of accountability disposition

Perceived organizational support, as conceptualized by Eisenberger et al. (1986), is one of the most influential predictors of employees' work attitudes and behavior. Organizational support has a unique relevance to accountability, given the nature of accountability as an interactive phenomenon, normally between subordinate and supervisor whose support is needed. In addition, the inclusion of organizational support in the present study helped to highlight the contribution of the main study variables – cultural values – to accountability. This was achieved by examining the predictability of the cultural values above and beyond that of organizational support (see the previous discussion on the predictive value of collectivism compared to organizational support) and the contribution of the interaction between the two. For teachers, organizational support referred in the study questionnaire to *school* support on both individual and school level (hierarchical model), while for principals it was *school board* support (multivariate regression model).

The expectation that organizational support would be related to accountability was met in the present study in the case of teachers. Results showed that organizational support was significantly related to both teacher external and internal accountability as well as to audience-focused (parents, school management) external accountability on the individual-teacher level, and both when principals' accountability was added to the analytic model or not added (Tables 4.37 and 4.38, respectively). These results are generally in line with past research on accountability and attitudes toward work. Two such studies showed that organizational support was related to felt accountability (Candra-Dewi & Riantoputra, 2019; Wikhamn & Hall, 2014).

Exchange Theory (Blau, 1964) combined with Gouldner's (1960) Reciprocity Theory may explain teacher external accountability to school management as reciprocal behavior, where teachers willingly tend to be accountable in exchange for perceived care and support on the part of the focal audience (school management). These reciprocal relations were not present in the parents' case. Rewards that come from parents are scarcely attached to concrete benefits and promotion, thus are probably less motivating at work and only slightly relevant to school support. This is perhaps the reason no relations were found for teachers between school support and external accountability on school level (which is the professional collective of teachers). It should be noted, though, that the interaction of collectivism and school support on the faculty level did predict external accountability to parents. Possibly, the embracing effect of group collectivism, that may see parents as included in school community, overcame teachers' non-recognition of parents' legitimacy, leading to accountability to parents.

With regard to principals, indeed, organizational (board) support correlated significantly with both accountability dimensions (Table 4.39), although regression analysis (Table 4.40) did not find a direct relation of organizational support to either external or internal accountability, not even when external accountability was targeted toward the two specific audiences (Table 4.42). Results also showed a significant negative relation between the interaction of individualism and organizational support to external accountability ($\beta=-0.22$, $p < .05$). In other words, the less principals felt that their personal and professional needs for organizational support were fulfilled, the more their adherence to individualistic values led to increased external accountability, or the more they perceived themselves receiving organizational support, the weaker was the relation between individualism and accountability. Apparently, as described in the section on cultural values, organizational support could compensate for lower accountability due to low individualism scores. However, when external accountability was focused on the two audiences – parents and school management – the higher (not lower) support they experienced from managerial boards, the higher were relations between their collectivist values and accountability. These results raised questions, addressed next, concerning the contrast between the different predictability directions (enhancing or hindering accountability), the different roles of individualism and collectivism in the presence of organizational support in the case of principals' accountability, and the results regarding principals' general accountability compared to their audience-focused accountability.

It is possible that principals who experienced little support from school boards felt that they were left alone to be held individually accountable for school performance. Lack of support may have elicited principals' individualistic aspirations to survive and succeed at work by emphasizing their accountability. When accountability for school failure (as well as success) could not be shared by other administrative position-holders, individualistic (and not collectivistic) values led principals to willingly (and realistically) accept external accountability. However, when the accountability audience was defined by a specific school collective (parents or school management), their collectivist, not individualist, values led to higher external accountability. It is possible that specific audiences raised higher collectivistic levels of commitment among principals because accountability had a clear target. These results may attenuate and calibrate theories arguing that employees in individualistic cultures would tend to be accountable more than those in collectivist cultures (Gelfand et al., 2004; Velayutham & Perera, 2004). Our results showed that organizational support interacted with individualism (principals) and collectivism (teachers) to affect accountability disposition. Organizational support, then, affected the way cultural values related to accountability.

Country similarities and differences in organizational support

Although the scores on organizational support do not vary widely among countries (Figure 4.9), the MANOVA showed a considerable amount of variance explained by country: 16% for teachers and 40% for principals (Chapter 4, p. 99). These amounts of variance came mainly from one country in each sample having a rather different score from most other countries: in the case of teachers, *China* was extreme, while for principals it was *Spain*. The position of *Spain* was discussed previously and is consistent with the results from the TALIS 2018 study (OECD, 2019). Unfortunately, *China* did not participate in this TALIS study. It seems plausible that the *China* teachers' experience of low organizational support was connected to the country's Confucian tradition with a strong emphasis on hierarchy and compliance with obligations and rules. In *China*, teachers work in their own classrooms with very little communication with their colleagues and feelings of loneliness may result from that (e.g., Rasmussen & Zou, 2014).

Organizational support and background variables

Finally, background-variable analysis showed that organizational support seemed to be stable vis-à-vis gender: no gender differences were found for either teachers or principals. Seniority, though, had different effects for the two study samples: while correlation between organizational support and seniority was positive (though small) for teachers ($r=.078$, $p < .05$), it was insignificant for principals. Apparently, as teachers gain more experience at work they report on some increased organizational support, while seniority for principals did not make a difference in their experience of board support. These findings may attest to the strong influence of school support on teachers' attitudes to work, with little dependence on background factors, an effect that does not exist for principals, whose sense of accountability is less dependent on organizational support to start with.

In sum, organizational support was found in the present study to be a potent job factor that is significantly related to accountability disposition directly and (when interacted with cultural values) indirectly. These results are supported by organizational-behavior literature on the powerful effect of organizational support in employees' work life. Although the role of organizational support in the present culture-focused study was mostly methodological (to highlight the effect of cultural values), these results added to our understanding of the important value of organizational support in securing teachers and principals' tendency to be externally and internally accountable. As accountability depends strongly on employee integrity and honesty, perceived organizational support encourages transparent work reports and acceptance of true feedback from superiors – both essential pillars of accountability.

6 Concluding thoughts

The study described in this book showed that educators' perceived accountability varied widely among individuals and among teacher-faculty groups, which alludes to the credibility of research on accountability as an individual difference. In this chapter, we conclude with observations based on the present study results and the way they were interpreted, while considering the relevant literature background. We focus particularly on the theoretical and practical implications of our study and offer some suggestions for continuing future research.

Educators' accountability versus school accountability

The present study focused on accountability as a subjective manifestation of teachers' and principals' accountability at work. This perspective filled a lacuna of research and practice on school accountability in the last two decades or so. Surprisingly, although school educators' reactions to accountability policy and regulation have been reported extensively in academic forums (e.g., Dizon-Ross, 2020; Erichsen & Reynolds, 2020), little research has been conducted on educators' own perceived accountability. To us, the individuals' subjective accountability seemed to be an inseparable part of institutional accountability regarding students' academic and social outcomes. The reason we considered perceived accountability as an essential part of school accountability is that teachers and principals are at the forefront of the educational endeavor. We found it only natural to seek consistency and harmony between institutional accountability and its individuals' perceived accountability, in other words to seek a person-organization fit (Kristof, 1996). We hope that our study will enhance a holistic view of school accountability consisting of bureaucratic regulation as well as educators' inherent accountability conviction.

Examples of poor relations between educators' accountability and institutional accountability are evident in the literature focusing on the implications of school accountability policy on teachers' work life. School accountability standards are typically designed and implemented by bureaucratic processes and regulations. Often, as reported in numerous studies, reactions of teachers involved in school actions to exhibit accountability were characterized by symptoms such as lower morale, tendency to leave (Erichsen & Reynolds, 2020), resentment of work evaluation (Moran, 2017), and stress (Shaw, 2016). These reactions, ironically, may be the result of a rather passive role given to educators who are at the center of accountability actions. In Elmore's (2005) words, individual values should align with collective expectations to create internal accountability. It is likely, then, that in those organizations where individuals and global forces work in harmony toward the establishment of a sound accountability policy, and the focus of accountability rests no less on educators' professional skills than on bureaucratic and political aspirations (Müller & Hernández, 2010), the chances of participants' negative responses would be more remote.

It follows that knowledge about individuals' accountability disposition may contribute to the design and implementation of school accountability policy. Of course, to ensure the desired match between accountability policy and individuals' attitudes and behavior, it would be important to set in place a safe environment for educators, where transparent and honest work reports are possible. Such accountability environments should consider needed effective school support and trustworthy mechanisms for work report, performance assessment, and rewards and sanctions (Frink & Ferris, 1998).

Focus on internal accountability

Researchers of individual accountability in education distinguished between external and internal accountability (e.g., Firestone & Shipps, 2005; Poulson, 1998). We focus here on internal accountability because we believe it carries some remedies for the ills and pitfalls of school accountability. Moreover, we maintain that the values behind internal accountability should shape future school accountability.

Two factors are at the heart of the distinction between the two accountability dimensions: one, the nature of the audience that receives work reports, and two, the values underlying the relationships between the agent and the audience. In external accountability, the audience is a relevant school stakeholder different from the agent, whereas in internal accountability, the two bodies (agent and audience) are in fact embodied in one person. As for underlying values, external accountability is led by values such as obedience to rules, compliance with the law, and loyalty to management. Internal accountability, on the other hand, is motivated by adherence to professional standards and to individual and shared ethical values. One's external accountability then may be viewed as a mere subjective image (personal response) of the formal accountability regulation system. Internal accountability, on the other hand, is an authentic conviction of one's responsibility to embrace the highest inner standards at work.

Given the abstract nature of internal accountability, and the fact that it is not the formal type by which accountability is commonly known, we believe that studying it is a key contribution of the present study. As defined here, internal accountability corresponds with a call coming from educational scholars (e.g., Darling-Hammond & Snyder, 2015; Snyder & Bristol, 2015) for a professional, not bureaucracy-based, accountability. Similarly, Sugrue and Sefika (2017) advanced the notion of professional accountability (distinguished from political accountability) that is defined as being responsible for one's own behavior, providing service for others' benefit. Considering the almost unconditional criticism that confronted accountability policies such as the U.S. *No Child Left Behind Act* and the British *Accountability Policy* (Keddie, 2015), internal accountability in the form of professional accountability seems the best hope for the future.

Our study results showed that both teachers and principals rated themselves as significantly more internally than externally accountable. As a self-report score, it is clear that this is the way they saw themselves, or the way they wanted to be seen. It is encouraging to realize educators believed more strongly in the importance of professional than bureaucratic values at work. Policy makers may be interested in these results and design ways to channel teachers' and principals' perception of internal accountability into practices that put an emphasis on professional skills and more collaborative relations with their students, management, parents, and other relevant school audiences. Interestingly, teacher internal (and not external) accountability was predicted among teachers in our study by individualistic values. This finding implies that educators' individualistic values may contribute to work quality, provided that individualist teachers' inspiration for success is focused on intrinsic values such as professional achievements and morality.

Cultural values and accountability – theoretical and practical implications

The present study focused on cultural values, individualism and collectivism, as predictors of accountability. Theoretically, the study findings corroborated previous results on the relations of the two values to a host of organizational attitudes and behaviors (e.g., Gelfand et al., 2007; Triandis,

1995, 2001). Our study results then contributed to the development of the theory of cultural values, applying it to the educational context. We showed that collectivism predicted teachers' and principals' external and internal accountability. Individualism predicted internal accountability among teachers and external accountability among principals.

In addition to the theoretical contribution to Accountability Theory, we believe that these results have practical implications to the educational field. Following social processes like overseas relocation, expatriate settlement, international partnerships, immigration, and fleeing of refugees, the field of education has expanded to respond to new challenges, crossing geographic and cultural borders (Choo, 2017). Children of refugees and new immigrants are joining schools in foreign countries, and educators move more easily overseas and serve as teachers in new countries. The increasing human mobility in many parts of the world should draw attention to the importance of the cultural imperative in schools and educational enterprises. Recognition of the fundamental cultural values, beliefs, conceptions, and life perspectives of educators may contribute to the understanding of different forms of individuals' accountability at work. Specifically, the present study applied knowledge on the effect of individualism and collectivism to accountability in education, both as an individual and as a country attribute.

The study results highlighted, as well, the dominance of collectivism over individualism among teachers and principals in relationship to accountability. This result is in contrast to theories by Gelfand et al. (2004) and Velayutham and Perera (2004) that argued for individualism as the stronger predictor of organizational behavior. With reference to theories of schools as community environments (Fullan et al., 2015; Starrat, 2007), our results imply that enhancing the sense of collectivism among teacher faculty and principals may elevate both external and internal accountability. Schools could try to adopt programs to nurture the sense of collectivism among all stakeholders – teachers, management, students, parents, support employees, and relevant community members. At the same time, individualistic values should not be played down due to their important relationship with internal accountability. Individualism also should be nurtured, as long as individualistic values such as achievement orientation reflect not only personal advancement but also point toward professional goals to the benefit of students and schools.

The contingent role of the accountability audience

One of the lesser-studied topics in accountability research is accountability audience. Although accountability disposition is expected to be a solid personal attribute, we found in the present study that teachers' and principals' accountability varied considerably between the different audiences, and that each of the two groups of educators, teachers, and principals was different in regard to its accountability level toward each of the two audiences studied. Apparently, even as a personal disposition, accountability is not a solid virtue; more accurately, it has a situational component contingent on the focal stakeholder and other situational factors, such as country affiliation. The audience most interesting to us was parents because this inherent stakeholder unit is seldom recognized formally as an audience entitled to get reports from teachers and principals. Rather, the legitimacy of this audience has often been controversial (Addi-Raccah & Grinshtain, 2018; Egger et al., 2015). This teachers' attitude of reserve toward school parents is in contrast with the reality of growing parental involvement in school life (Vincent & Ball, 2006). We, therefore, compared teachers' and principals' accountability disposition toward parents and school management and found that both external and internal accountability of the two educator groups to school management were significantly and substantially higher than it was to parents.

The practical implication of this across-the-board finding is particularly prominent because formal mechanisms to ensure accountability seldom exist in regard to parents (Addi-Raccah & Grinshtain, 2018); thus, little documentation has been retained. If school policy is focused on encouraging teachers to report to such non-managerial audiences, mechanisms for assessing and channeling accountability in these cases should be tailored to the situation. Also, professional training is needed to establish accountability standards for non-managerial school stakeholders and to support teachers' recognition of the legitimacy of such groups to be informed of school outcomes. This type of accountability is formally external, being directed to parties external to the focal agent (Firestone & Shipps, 2005), but at the same time also internal, reflecting professional responsibility on the part of teachers and school administrators (Darling-Hammond & Snyder, 2015; Firestone & Shipps, 2005; Sugrue & Sefika, 2017).

Our results also imply that audiences other than parents not commonly mentioned in regard to teachers' and principals' accountability should be considered. These could be any non-managerial audiences in the school environment (e.g., students, community members). Our recommendation to researchers is to draw attention to possible combinations of school agents and audiences, such as teacher-student, teacher-teacher colleagues, principal-school faculty, or principal-town populace. Each of these dyads may constitute a solid and relevant ground to form a unique type of accountability, leaning on social, professional, and ethical values. These new forms of accountability have the potential to solidify school work toward a holistic view of the educational mission.

Team accountability: a future research direction

The present study is focused on accountability as a subjective individual characteristic. However, our results indicate that accountability may take a collective form, namely, it may characterize groups, not only individuals, and we therefore suggest investigating, in future studies, accountability also as a group phenomenon. We base our recommendation on the following findings and observations pointing to the importance of group-level indicators.

First, while using the HLM two-level analysis, we found that *group level* (in this case school faculty) variables were unexpectedly significantly related to *teacher faculty's* internal and external accountability. When comparing the individual with the group-level-explained variance of our independent variables (culture and organizational support), the latter level showed a considerably larger effect than the former. More specifically, we found that teacher faculty-level individualism, collectivism, and organizational support explained between two to four times as much of the variance in teacher accountability than the teachers' individual variables. We would like to emphasize that this comparison is relative to the (explained) variances located on corresponding (individual and faculty) levels. In other words, accountability variance between schools was higher than that within a given school.

Second, our results showed clearly that cultural values (individualism, collectivism) were predictors of accountability among teachers and principals. Our explanation of these results drew from the interactive nature of accountability, where two parties interrelate within a universe of dense networks among parties, such as teachers, students, school management, and parents. It follows that accountability, which involves social interchange, may characterize not only a given individual but also a group of individuals who are members of the same network.

Third, studies on the relations between accountability and cultural values showed that collectivist societies promote accountability at a group level. Gelfand et al. (2004), for example, argued that in collectivistic societies, in contrast to individualistic ones, accountability would tend to rest with the group, not with individuals. Velayutham and Perera (2004) contended that people in collectivist societies would be more accountable than in individualist societies. This line of research implies that accountability may be typical of groups that are characterized by a shared cultural value, such as collectivism, and thus may appear and be examined as a group feature. Interestingly, social loafing, which is one's tendency to decrease performance when working in a group, was found more prominent among individualists than collectivists in a comparative study between U.S. and Chinese workers

(Earley, 1989). Social loafing in this study decreased in a collectivist society characterized by enhanced accountability for performance.

Fourth, the team structure in many work organizations suggests that accountability may necessarily be attributed to more than one person. When actions taken at work do not result in success, an employee performance report is likely to be accompanied by explanations and excuses (Hareli et al., 2005; Shaw et al., 2003). Theories about account-giving in accountability contexts may not be relevant in schools that typically consist of closely-tight professional communities (Smetackova et al., 2020; Starrat, 2007). Each school student is normally surrounded by a team of teachers and educators at any given moment (e.g., subject-matter teacher, homeroom teacher, class-level coordinator, pedagogic coordinator, counselor). Working in collaboration, their influence on students' education is roughly simultaneous at any given point in school time. Instruction and education in general never start at a specific moment but normally constitute a continuous process. Holding a given teacher solely accountable for students' academic or social outcomes, accordingly, is not likely to be realistic. It follows that, in the case of school education, accountability is likely to be shared at any point by more than one person, thus shared by a work team.

Finally, the perception of accountability as a group phenomenon also draws from the Social Contagion Theory (Burgess et al., 2018). Teachers may influence not only students but also each other when working as a team, while developing a group accountability climate similarly to other types of organizational climates, such as safety climate (Zohar & Luria, 2005), job security climate (Sora et al., 2013), and justice climate (Herr et al., 2018). Research that advances the idea of accountability climate in schools may contribute to a better understanding of this multi-faceted concept that seems to affect schools so profoundly.

To conclude, research on team accountability would complement the evolving research, of which the present study is part, about perceived individual accountability. We believe that in accountability policy, a stronger emphasis than usual on team accountability may enhance educators' positive approach to both external and internal accountability. Future studies may also investigate whether introducing team accountability helps to remove some of the detrimental effects of individual accountability.

References

Addi-Raccah, A., & Friedman, N. (2019). A liminal approach to parents in leadership positions in schools with students of high socioeconomic background in Israel. *Journal of Educational Administration, 58*(1), 96–111.
Addi-Raccah, A., & Grinshtain, Y. (2018). Teachers' capital in view of intensive parental involvement in school: The case of teachers in high socio-economic status schools in Israel. *Research Papers in Education, 33*(5), 599–619.
Ambrosio, J. (2013). Changing the subject: Neoliberalism and accountability in public education. *Educational Studies: Journal of the American Educational Studies Association, 49*(4), 316–333.
Amrein-Beardsley, A., & Holloway, J. (2019). Value-added models for teacher evaluation and accountability: Commonsense assumptions. *Educational Policy, 33*(3), 516–542.
Anastasiou, S., & Papagianni, A. (2020). Parents, teachers and principals views on parental involvement in secondary schools. *Education Sciences, 10*(69), 1–12.
Aria, A., Jafari, B., & Behifar, M. (2019). Authentic leadership and teachers' intention to stay: The mediating role of perceived organizational support and psychological capital. *World Journal of Education, 9*(3), 67–81.
Bæck, U. D. K. (2010). 'We are the professionals': A study of teachers' views on parental involvement in school. *British Journal of Sociology of Education, 31*(3), 323–335.
Baskerville, R. F. (2003). Hofstede never studied culture. *Accounting, Organizations and Society, 28*(1), 1–14.
Berkovich, I. (2019). Educational governance transition in a social democratic country: A process-tracing analysis. *Journal of Educational Change, 20*, 193–219.
Beugelsdijk, S., & Welzel, C. (2018). Dimensions and dynamics of national culture: Synthesizing Hofstede with Inglehart. *Journal of Cross-Cultural Psychology, 49*(10), 1469–1505.
Bibi, A., Khalid, M. A., & Hussain, A. (2019). Perceived organizational support and organizational commitment among special education teachers in Pakistan. *International Journal of Educational Management, 33*(5), 848–859.
Bibu, N., & Saris, H. (2017). Managing the process of stakeholders involvement in junior high-schools in Arab sector in Israel, and its effects on pupils, teachers and parents. *Review of International Comparative Management, 18*(2), 200–217.

References

Blau, P. (1964). *Power and exchange in social life*. New York: John Wiley and Sons.
Booyse, J. (2015). *Aspects of the new accountability regime in South Africa*. Paper presented at the ECER, Budapest.
Brandts, J., & Garofalo, O. (2012). Gender pairings and accountability effects. *Journal of Economic Behavior & Organization, 83*, 31–41.
Burgess, L. G., Riddell, P. M., Fancourt, A., & Murayama, K. (2018). The influence of social contagion within education: Motivational perspective. *Mind, Brain & Education, 12*(4), 164–174.
Candra-Dewi, R., & Riantoputra, C. (2019). Felt accountability: The role of personality and organizational factors. *Journal of Managerial Development, 38*(4), 312–322.
Chan, T. C., Jiang, B., Chandler, M., Morris, R., Slawomir, R., Turan, S., Shu, Z., & Kpeglo, S. (2019). School principals self-perceptions of their roles and responsibilities in six countries. *New Waves Educational Research and Development, 22*(2), 37–61.
Chang, Y., Leach, N., & Anderman, E. M. (2015). The role of perceived autonomy support in principals' affective organizational commitment and job satisfaction. *Social Psychology of Education, 18*, 315–336.
Chidozie, N. R. (2017). *Accountability in the education section of South Africa. Global education monitoring report*. Paris: UNESCO.
Choo, S. S. (2017). Global education and its tensions: Case studies of two schools in Singapore and US. *Asian Pacific Journal of Education, 37*(4), 552–566.
Cochran-Smith, M., Stringer-Keefe, E., Burton, S., Chang, W.-C., Fernandez, M. B., Miller, A. F., Sanchez, J. G., & Baker, M. (2018). *Reclaiming accountability in teacher education*. New York: Teachers College Press.
Coget, J.-F. (2011). Does managerial motivation spill over to subordinates? *Academy of Management Perspectives, 25*(4), 84–85.
Cohen, J. (1988). *Statistical power analysis for the behavioral sciences* (2nd ed.). Hillsdale, NJ: Lawrence Erlbaum Associates.
Conway, S. L., O'Keefe, P. A., & Hrasky, S. L. (2015). Legitimacy, accountability and impression management in NGO's: The Indian Ocean tsunami. *Accounting, Auditing and Accountability, 28*(7), 1075–1098.
Darling-Hammond, L. (2007). Race, inequality and educational accountability: The irony of 'No Child Left Behind.' *Race Ethnicity and Education, 10*(3), 245–260.
Darling-Hammond, L., & Ascher, C. (1991). *Accountability mechanisms in big city school systems*. ERIC/CUE Digest No. 71.
Darling-Hammond, L., & Snyder, J. (2015). Meaningful learning in a new paradigm for educational accountability: An introduction. *Educational Policy Analysis Archives, 23*(7), 1–8.
Davis, E., Davern, M., Waters, E., Boyd, R., Reddihough, D., Mackinnon, A., & Graham, H. K. (2013). *Cerebral palsy quality of life questionnaire for adolescents (CP QOL-teen) manual*. Melbourne: University of Melbourne.
Davis-Blake, A., & Pfeffer, J. (1989). Just a mirage: The search for dispositional effects in organizational research. *Academy of Management Review, 14*(3), 385–400.

Dizon-Ross, R. (2020). How does school accountability affect teachers? Evidence from New York City. *Journal of Human Resources*, *55*(1), 76–118.

Drach-Zahavi, A., Leonenko, M., & Srulovici, E. (2018). Towards a measure of accountability in nursing: A three-way validation study. *Journal of Advanced Nursing*, *74*(10), 2450–2464.

Dubnick, M. J. (2003). Accountability and ethics: Reconsidering their relationships. *International Journal of Organizational Theory and Behavior*, *6*(3), 405–441.

Dubrin, A. J. (2011). *Impression management in the workplace: Research, theory and practice*. New York: Routledge.

Earley, P. C. (1989). Social loafing and collectivism: A comparison of the United States and the People's Republic of China. *Administrative Science Quarterly*, *34*(4), 565–581.

Easley, J. II, & Tulowitzki, P. (2016). *Educational accountability: International perspectives on challenges and possibilities for school leadership*. London: Routledge.

Egger, J., Lehmann, J., & Straumann, M. (2015). "Collaboration with parents isn't a burden. Its just a natural part of my work." Parental involvement in Switzerland – an analysis of attitudes and practices of Swiss primary school teachers. *International Journal About Parents in Education*, *9*(1), 119–130.

Ehren, M. C., & Shackleton, N. (2016). Risk-based school inspections: Impact of targeted inspection approaches on Dutch secondary schools. *Educational Assessment, Evaluation and Accountability*, *28*(4), 299–321.

Eisenberger, R., Huntington, R., Hutchison, S., & Sowa, D. (1986). Perceived organizational support. *Journal of Applied Psychology*, *71*(3), 500–507.

Eisenberger, R., Shanock, L. R., & Wen, X. (2020). Perceived organizational support: Why caring about employees counts. *Annual Review of Organizational Psychology and Organizational Behavior*, *7*(1), 101–124.

Elmore, R. F. (2005). Accountable leadership. *The Educational Forum*, *69*(2), 134–142.

Enders, C. K., & Tofighi, D. (2007). Centering predictor variables in cross-sectional multilevel models: A new look at an old issue. *Psychological Methods*, *12*(2), 121.

Eraut, M. (1993). Teacher accountability: Why is it central in teacher professional development? In L. Kremer-Hayon, H. C. Vonk, & R. Fessler (Eds.), *Teacher professional development: A multiple perspective approach* (pp. 23–43). Amsterdam: Swets and Zeitlinger.

Erez, M., & Earley, P. C. (1993). *Culture, self-identity and work*. New York: Oxford University Press.

Erichsen, K., & Reynolds, J. (2020). Public school accountability, workplace culture and teacher morale. *Social Science Research*, *85*, 1–15.

ESSA (Every Student Succeeds Act of 2015). U.S. Public Law 114–95.

Farooqi, M. T. K., Ahmed, S., & Ashiq, I. (2019). Relationship of perceived organizational support with secondary school teachers' performance. *Bulletin of Education and Research*, *41*(3), 141–152.

Ferris, G. R., Dulebohn, J. H., Frink, D. D., George-Falvy, J., Mitchell, T. R., & Matthews, L. M. (1997). Job and organizational characteristics, accountability, and employee influence. *Journal of Managerial Issues, 9*(2), 162–175.

Firestone, W. A., & Shipps, D. (2005). How do leaders interpret conflicting accountabilities to improve student learning? In C. Riehl & W. Firestone (Eds.), *A new agenda: Directions for research on educational leadership* (pp. 81–100). New York: Teachers College Press.

Freeman, R., Harrison, J., Wicks, A., Parmar, B., & de Colle, S. (2010). *Stakeholder theory: The state of the art*. Cambridge, UK: Cambridge University Press.

Frink, D. D., & Ferris, G. R. (1998). Accountability, impression management, and goal setting in the performance evaluation process. *Human Relations, 51*(10), 1259–1283.

Frink, D. D., & Klimoski, R. J. (1998). Toward a theory of accountability in organizations and human resource management. In G. R. Ferris (Ed.), *Research in personnel and human resources management* (Vol. 16, pp. 1–15). Edinburgh, London & Oxford, UK and Amsterdam, the Netherlands: Elsevier Science/JAI Press.

Fullan, M., Rincón-Gallardo, S., & Hargreaves, A. (2015). Professional capital as accountability. *Education Policy Annual Archives, 23*(15), 1–18.

Furman, G. C. (Ed.). (2002). *School as community: From promise to practice*. New York: State University of New York Press.

Gardner, W. C., & Martinko, M. J. (1988). Impression management: An observational study lining audience characteristics with verbal self-representation. *Academy of Management Journal, 31*(1), 42–85.

Gelfand, M. J., Erez, M., & Aycan, Z. (2007). Cross-cultural organizational behavior. *Annual Review of Psychology, 58*, 479–514.

Gelfand, M. J., Lim, B. C., & Raver, J. L. (2004). Culture and accountability in organizations: Variations in forms of social control across cultures. *Human Resource Management Review, 14*(1), 135–160.

Gelfand, M. J., & Realo, A. (1999). Individualism – collectivism and accountability in intergroup negotiations. *Journal of Applied Psychology, 84*(5), 721–736.

Gibton, D. (2011). Post-2000 law-based educational governance in Israel: Equality vs. diversity? *Educational Management, Administration and Leadership, 39*(4), 434–454.

Gouldner, A. (1960). The norm of reciprocity. *American Sociological Review, 25*(2), 161–178.

Greenfield, P. M. (2014). Sociodemographic differences within countries produce variable cultural values. *Journal of Cross-Cultural Psychology, 45*(1), 37–41.

Grinshtain, Y., & Gibton, D. (2018). Responsibility, authority and accountability in school-based and non-school-based management. *Journal of Educational Administration, 56*(1), 2–17.

Hall, A. T., Bowen, M. G., Ferris, G. R., Royle, M. T., & Fitzgibbons, D. E. (2007). The accountability lens: A new way to view management issues. *Business Horizons, 50*(5), 405–413.

Hall, A. T., & Ferris, G. R. (2011). Accountability and extra-role behavior. *Employee Responsibilities and Rights Journal, 23*(2), 131–144.

Hall, A. T., Frink, D. D., & Buckley, M. R. (2017). An accountability account: A review and synthesis of the theoretical and empirical research on felt accountability. *Journal of Organizational Behavior, 38*(2), 204–224.

Hall, A. T., Zinko, R., Perryman, A. A., & Ferris, G. R. (2009). Organizational citizenship behavior and reputation mediators in the relationships between accountability and job performance and satisfaction. *Journal of Leadership & Organizational Studies, 15*(4), 381–392.

Hallinger, P., Gümüş, S., & Bellibaş, M. Ş. (2020). 'Are principals instructional leaders yet?' A science map of the knowledge base on instructional leadership, 1940–2018. *Scientometrics, 122*(3), 1629–1650.

Hareli, S., Shomrat, N., & Biger, N. (2005). The role of emotions in employees' explanations for failure in the workplace. *Journal of Managerial Psychology, 20*(8), 663–680.

Heintz, P., & Steele-Johnson, D. (2004). Clarifying the conceptual definitions of goal orientation dimensions: Competence, control and evaluation. *Organizational Analysis, 12*(1), 5–19.

Herr, R. M., Bosch, J. A., Loerbroks, A., Genser, P., Almer, C., Van Vianen, A. E. M., & Fischer, J. E. (2018). Organizational justice, justice climate and somatic complaints: A multilevel investigation. *Journal of Psychosomatic Research, 111*, 15–21.

Hochwarter, W., Perrewe, P., Hall, A., & Ferris, G. (2005). Negative affectivity as a moderator of the form and magnitude of the relationship between felt accountability and job tension. *Journal of Organizational Behavior, 26*(5), 517–534.

Hofstede, G. (1983). The cultural relativity of organizational practices and theories. *Journal of International Business Studies, 14*(2), 75–89.

Hofstede, G. (2011). Dimensionalizing cultures: The Hofstede model in context. *Online Readings in Psychology and Culture, 2*(1). https://scholarworks.gvsu.edu/orpc/vol2/iss1/8/

Hofstede, G., Hofstede, G. J., & Minkow, M. (2010). *Cultures and organizations: Software of the mind* (3rd ed.). New York: McGraw-Hill.

Hornby, G., & Lafaele, R. (2011). Barriers to parental involvement in education: An explanatory model. *Educational Review, 63*(1), 37–52.

House, R. J., Dorfman, P. W., Javidan, M., Hanges, P. J., & de Luque, M. F. S. (2014). *Strategic leadership across cultures: The GLOBE study of CEO leadership behavior and effectiveness in 24 countries.* Thousand Oaks, CA: Sage.

House, R. J., Hanges, P. J., Javidan, M., Dorfman, P. W., & Gupta, V. (Eds.). (2004). *Culture, leadership, and organizations: The GLOBE study of 62 societies.* Thousand Oaks, CA: Sage.

Hox, J. J., Moerbeek, M., & Van de Schoot, R. (2017). *Multilevel analysis: Techniques and applications.* New York: Routledge.

IBM Corp. (2017). *IBM SPSS Statistics for Windows, Version 25.0 [Computer software].* Armonk, NY: IBM Corp.

Jiang, H. (2016). Revisiting individualism and collectivism: A multinational examination of pre-service teachers' perceptions on student academic performances. *Journal of Intercultural Education, 27*(1), 101–110.

Keddie, A. (2015). School autonomy, accountability and collaboration: A critical review. *Journal of Educational Administration and History*, *47*(1), 1–17.

Khanolainen, D. (2019). Attitudes of Russian teachers towards the new standards. *Quality Assurance in Education*, *27*(3), 254–268.

Kim, U. (1995). *Individualism and collectivism: A psychological, cultural and ecological analysis*. Nordic Institute of Asian Studies (NIAS) Report series (No. 21).

Knapp, M. S., & Feldman, S. B. (2012). Managing the intersection of internal and external accountability. *Journal of Educational Administration*, *50*(5), 666–694.

Krejsler, J. (2005). Professions and their identities: How to explore professional development among (semi-) professions. *Scandinavian Journal of Educational Research*, *49*(4), 335–357.

Kristof, A. L. (1996). Person-organization fit: An integrative review of its conceptualization, measurement and implication. *Personnel Psychology*, *49*(1), 1–49.

Laird, C. (1971). *Webster's new world thesaurus*. New York: Simon & Schuster.

Lareau, A., & Muñoz, V. L. (2012). "You're not going to call the shots" – structural conflicts between the principal and the PTO at a suburban public elementary school. *Sociology of Education*, *85*(3), 201–218.

Larson, R. B. (2019). Controlling social desirability bias. *International Journal of Market Research*, *61*(5), 534–547.

Lavrakas, P. J. (2008). *Encyclopedia of survey research methods* (Vol. 1). Thousand Oaks, CA: Sage.

Lee, J., & Wong, K. K. (2004). The impact of accountability on racial and socioeconomic equity: Considering both school resources and achievement outcomes. *American Educational Research Journal*, *41*(4), 797–832.

Leng, C.-H., Huang, H.-Y., & Yao, G. (2020). A social desirability item response theory model: Retrieve-deceive-transfer. *Psychometrika*, *85*(1), 56–74.

Leonenko, M., & Drach-Zahavy, A. (2016). You are either on the court or sitting on the bench: Understanding accountability from the perspectives of nurses and nursing managers. *Journal of Advanced Nursing*, *72*(11), 2718–2727.

Lerner, J. S., & Tetlock, P. E. (1999). Accounting for the effects of accountability. *Psychological Bulletin*, *125*(2), 255–275.

Liu, Y., & Bellibas, M. S. (2018). School factors that are related to school principals' job satisfaction and organizational commitment. *International Journal of Educational Research*, *90*, 1–19.

Lortie, D. C. (2009). *School principal: Managing in public*. Chicago: The University of Chicago Press.

Maas, C. J., & Hox, J. J. (2005). Sufficient sample sizes for multilevel modeling. *Methodology*, *1*(3), 86–92.

Markus, H., & Kitayama, S. (1991). Culture and the self: Implications for cognition, emotion, and motivation. *Psychological Review*, *98*(2), 224–253.

Menlo, A., Collet, L., Rosenblatt, Z., Williamson, J., & Wubbels, T. (Eds.). (2015). *Do teachers wish to be agents of change?* Rotterdam: Sense Publishers.

Meyers, M. C., Adams, B. G., Sekaja, L., Buzea, C., Cazan, A. M., Gotea, M., . . . van Woerkom, M. (2019). Perceived organizational support for the use of employees' strengths and employee well-being: A cross-country comparison. *Journal of Happiness Studies*, *20*(6), 1825–1841.

Miller, M. J., Woehr, D. J., & Hudspeth, N. (2002). The meaning and measurement of work ethics: Construction and initial validation of a multi-dimensional inventory. *Journal of Vocational Behavior, 60*(3), 451–489.

Moran, R. M. R. (2017). The impact of a high-stakes teacher evaluation system: Educator perspectives on accountability. *Educational Studies, 53*(2), 178–193.

Mpungose, J. E., & Ngwenya, T. H. (2017). School leadership and accountability in managerialist times: Implications for South African public schools. *Education as Change, 21*(3), 1–16.

Müller, J., & Hernández, F. (2010). On the geography of accountability: Comparative analysis of teachers' experiences across seven European countries. *Journal of Educational Change, 11*, 307–322.

Nataly, P. D., Mukhneri, M., & Maruf, A. (2019). The effects of perceived organizational support and affective organization commitment on organizational citizenship behaviour of senior secondary teachers. *Indian Journal of Public Health Research & Development, 10*(1), 1281–1285.

National Commission on Excellence in Education. (1983). *A nation at risk: The imperative for educational reform.* Washington, DC: United States Government Printing Office.

NCLB (No Child Left Behind Act of 2002). U.S. Public Law 107–110.

OECD. (2003). *Education at a glance.* Paris: OECD Publishing.

OECD. (2019). *TALIS) 2018). Teachers and school leaders as lifelong learners.* Paris: OECD Publishing.

Oser, F. (1991). Professional morality: A discourse approach (the case of the teaching profession). In W. Kurtines & J. Gewirtz (Eds.), *Handbook of moral behavior and development* (Vol. 2, pp. 191–228). Hillsdale, NJ: Lawrence Erlbaum Associates.

Parimah, A., Davour, M. J., Kofi, C. C., & Winder, B. (2018). A restorative justice ideology among high school teachers in Ghana: Investigating the role of collectivism and personality. *Contemporary Justice Review, 21*(4), 420–431.

Pascual, M. A. C. (2009). The work values of teacher training students in a Spanish university. Symbiosis between Schwartz and meaning of work (MOW) study group. *European Journal of Education, 44*(3), 441–453.

Peeters, M., Zondervan-Zwijnenburg, M., Vink, G., & Van de Schoot, R. (2015). How to handle missing data: A comparison of different approaches. *European Journal of Developmental Psychology, 12*(4), 377–394.

Petty, G. C., & Hill, R. B. (1995). Work ethics characteristics: Perceived work ethics of supervisors and workers. *Journal of Industrial Teacher Education, 42*(2), 5–20.

Poppleton, P., & Williamson, J. (Eds.). (2004). *New realities of secondary teachers' work lives.* London: Symposium Books.

Poulson, L. (1998). Accountability, teacher professionalism and education reform in England. *Teacher Development, 2*(3), 419–432.

Rasmussen, P., & Zou, Y. (2014). The development of educational accountability in China and Denmark. *Education Policy Analysis Archives, 22*, 1–21.

Raudenbush, S. W., Bryk, A. S., & Congdon, R. (2004). *HLM 6 for Windows [Computer software].* Lincolnwood, IL: Scientific Software International.

References 161

Rhodes, L., & Eisenberger, R. (2002). Perceived organizational support: A review of the literature. *Journal of Applied Psychology, 87*, 698–714.

Roch, S. G., & McNall, L. A. (2007). An investigation of factors influencing accountability and performance ratings. *The Journal of Psychology, 141*(5), 499–523.

Rosenblatt, Z. (2017). Personal accountability in education: Measure development and validation. *Journal of Educational Administration, 55*(1), 18–32.

Rosenblatt, Z., & Shimoni, O. (2002). Teachers' accountability: An experimental field study in physical education. *Journal of Personnel Evaluation in Education, 15*(4), 309–328.

Schlenker, B. R., & Weigold, M. F. (1989). Self-identification and accountability. In R. A. Giacalone & P. Rosenfeld (Eds.), *Impression management in the organization* (pp. 21–43). Hillsdale, NJ: Erlbaum.

Schwartz, S. H. (1994). Beyond individualism-collectivism: New cultural dimensions of values. In U. Kim, H. C. Triandis, C. Kagitcibasi, S.-C. Choi, & G. Yoon (Eds.), *Individualism and collectivism: Theory, method, and application* (pp. 77–119). Newbury Park, CA: Sage.

Scott, J. A., & Halkias, D. (2016). Consensus processes fostering relational trust among stakeholder leaders in a middle school: A multi-case study. *International Leadership Study, 8*(3), 23–33.

Seashore-Louis, K., Febey, K., & Schroeder, R. (2005). State-mandated accountability in high-schools: Teachers' interpretations of a new era. *Educational Evaluation and Policy Analysis, 27*(2), 177–204.

Sezgin-Nartgün, S. (2017). Power sources at schools: Official and unofficial power. *International Online Journal of Educational Sciences, 9*(2), 561–574.

Shaw, J. C., Wild, E., & Colquitt, J. A. (2003). To justify or excuse? A meta-analytic review of the effect of explanation. *Journal of Applied Psychology, 88*, 444–458.

Shaw, R. D. (2016). Music teachers stress in the era of accountability. *Arts Education Policy Review, 117*(2), 104–116.

Smetackova, I., Viktorova, I., Lauermann, M., & Jones, C. (2020). Community schools in selected Eastern European and Eurasian countries: Implementation processes and results. *Peabody Journal of Education, 95*(1), 15–32.

Snyder, J., & Bristol, T. (2015). Professional accountability for improved life, college and career readiness. *Educational Policy Analysis Archives, 23*(16), 1–30.

Somech, A., & Wenderow, M. (2006). The impact of participative and directive leadership on teachers' performance: The intervening effects of job structuring, decision domain and leader-member exchange. *Educational Administration Quarterly, 42*(5), 746–772.

Sora, B., De Cuyper, N., Caballer, A., et al. (2013). Outcomes of job insecurity climate: The role of climate strength. *Applied Psychology: An International Review, 62*(3), 382–405.

Starrat, R. J. (2007). Leading a community of learners: Learning to be moral by engaging the morality learning. *Educational Management, Administration and Leadership, 35*(2), 165–183.

References

Staw, B. M., Bell, N. E., & Clausen, J. A. (1986). The dispositional approach to job attitudes: A lifetime longitudinal test. *Administrative Science Quarterly*, *31*(1), 56–77.

Staw, B. M., & Ross, J. (1985). Stability in the midst of change: A dispositional approach to job attitudes. *Journal of Applied Psychology*, *70*, 469–480.

Sugrue, C., & Sefika, M. S. (2017). Professional responsibility, accountability and performativity among teachers: The leavening influence of CPD? *Teachers and Teaching: Theory and Practice*, *23*(2), 171–190.

Teo, T., & Huang, F. (2019). Investigating the influence of individually espoused cultural values on teachers' intentions to use educational technologies in Chinese universities. *Interactive Learning Environments*, *27*(5–6), 813–829.

Tetlock, P. E. (1983). Accountability and complexity of thought. *Journal of Personality and Social Psychology*, *45*(1), 74–83.

Tetlock, P. E. (1992). The impact of accountability on judgment and choice: Toward a social contingency model. *Advances in Experimental Social Psychology*, *25*(3), 331–377.

Tetlock, P. E., & Boettger, R. (1994). Accountability amplifies the status quo effect when change creates victims. *Journal of Behavioral Decision Making*, *7*(1), 1–23.

Thoms, P., Dose, J., & Scott, K. (2002). Relationships between accountability, job satisfaction and trust. *Human Resource Development Quarterly*, *13*(3), 307–323.

Triandis, H. C. (1980). Reflections on trends in cross-cultural research. *Journal of Cross-Cultural Psychology*, *11*(1), 35–58.

Triandis, H. C. (1993). Collectivism and individualism as cultural syndromes. *Cross-Cultural Research*, *27*(3–4), 155–180.

Triandis, H. C. (1995). *Individualism and collectivism*. Boulder, CO: Westview.

Triandis, H. C. (2001). Individualism-collectivism and personality. *Journal of Personality*, *69*(6), 907–924.

Triandis, H. C. (2004). The many dimensions of culture. *The Academy of Management Executive (1993–2005)*, *18*(1), 88–93.

Triandis, H. C., & Gelfand, M. J. (1998). Converging evidence of horizontal and vertical individualism and collectivism. *Journal of Personality and Social Psychology*, *74*, 118–128.

Triandis, H. C., & Suh, E. M. (2002). Cultural influences on personality. *Annual Review of Psychology*, *53*(1), 133–160.

Valli, L., & Buese, D. (2007). The changing roles of teachers in an era of high-stakes accountability. *American Educational Research Journal*, *44*(3), 519–558.

Van Buuren, S. (2018). *Flexible imputation of missing data*. London: Chapman and Hall/CRC.

Velayutham, S., & Perera, H. B. (2004). The influence of emotions and culture on accountability and governance. *Corporate Governance*, *1*(1), 52–64.

Vincent, C., & Ball, S. J. (2006). *Childcare, choice and class practices: Middle class parents and their children*. New York: Routledge.

Wang, F., Pollock, K., & Hauseman, C. (2018). School principals' job satisfaction: The effects of work intensification. *Canadian Journal of Educational Administration and Policy*, *185*, 73–90.

References

Watson, P. J., & Morris, R. J. (2002). Individualist and collectivist values: Hypotheses suggested by Alexis de Tocqueville. *The Journal of Psychology, 136*(3), 263–271.

Weathers, J. M. (2011). Teacher community in urban elementary schools: The role of leadership and bureaucratic accountability. *Educational Policy Analysis Archives, 19*(3), 1–42.

Wikhamn, W., & Hall, A. T. (2014). Accountability and job satisfaction: Organizational support as a moderator. *Journal of Managerial Psychology, 29*(5), 458–471.

Wood, J. A., & Winston, B. E. (2007). Development of three scales to measure leader accountability. *Leadership & Organization Development Journal, 28*(2), 167–185.

Wubbels, T., & van Tartwijk, J. (2018). Dutch teacher and teacher education policies: Trends and ambiguities. In H. Niemi, A. Toom, A. Kallioniemi, & J. Lavonen (Eds.), *The teacher's role in the changing globalizing world* (pp. 63–77). Leiden: Brill Sense.

Yilmaz, K., Altinkurt, Y., & Ozciftci, E. (2016). The relationship between teachers' views about cultural values and critical pedagogy. *Eurasian Journal of Educational Research, 16*(66), 191–210.

Zamir, S. (2019). The polymeric model of school evaluation in the era of accountability. *Quality Assurance in Education, 27*(4), 401–411.

Zeinabadi, H. R. (2014). Principal-teachers high-quality exchange indicators and student achievement testing a model. *Journal of Educational Administration, 52*(3), 404–420.

Zohar, D., & Luria, G. (2005). A multilevel model of safety climate: Cross-level relationships between organization and group-level climates. *Journal of Applied Psychology, 90*(4), 616–628.

Index

Note: Page numbers in *italics* indicate a figure and page numbers in **bold** indicate a table on the corresponding page.

accountability: across countries 75–79, 135–137; agent(s) of 7–10, 12, 20, 129, 148, 151, 171; audience(s) of 4, 6, 7, 8, 10–11, 12, 13, 15, 21, 26, 28, 29, 74, 83–88, 101, 108–110, 114, 122, 124, 126, 128–131, 134, 135, 144, 145, 148–151; climate of 153; by country *76*; cycle of 13; definition of 1, 6–7; ethics of 11; external/internal, defined 9–12; measurement of 15–16; organizational support and 23, 143–145; personal 9; policy xix, 2–4, 9, 124, 136, 137, 147–149, 153; professional 137, 149; situational view of 15, 128–129, 151; system level 1, 2, 3, 8; theory of 4–5, 150; *see also* collectivism; felt accountability; individualism; objective accountability; perceived accountability; principals' accountability; subjective accountability; teachers' accountability
Addi-Raccah, A. 13, 14, 151
Ambrosio, J. 3
Amrein-Beardsley, A. 127
Anastasiou, S. 14
answerability 7–8, 11, 16
Aria, A. 23
Ascher, C. 137
autonomy 17, 24, 30; teacher 3, 24, 138

Bæck, U. D. K. 13–14
Ball, S. J. 13, 151
Baskerville, R. F. 22
Bellibas, M. S. 24
Berkovich, I. 136
Beugelsdijk, S. 22
Bibi, A. 23
Bibu, N. 13
Blau, P. 24, 144
Boettger, R. 15
Booyse, J. 136
Brandts, J. 4
Bristol, T. 149
Buese, D. 3
Burgess, L. G. 153

Canada: collectivism in *139*, *141*; data collection on 27, **27**; gender differences in accountability in 80, **80**, 81, 82, 95, 94; seniority and accountability in **83**; seniority and collectivism/individualism in **97**; teacher accountability in **75**, *76*, 78, **78**, **79**, 80, *79*, **83**, **110**, 111, 135–136; teacher accountability to parents/school management in 84, **85**, *85*; teacher collectivism/individualism in **85**, *85*, **92**, *93*, *94*, *135*, *136*; teacher organizational support in 97, **98**, 99, *99*, **100**
Candra-Dewi, R. 23, 144

Chan, T. C. 134
Chang, Y. 24
Chidozie, N. R. 136
China: collectivism in *139*, *141*; data collection on 27, **27**, 31; gender differences in accountability in **80**, **81**, 94, **95**; seniority and accountability in **83**; seniority and collectivism/individualism in **97**; teacher accountability in **75**, 76, 78, **78**, 79, 84, 135–136; teacher accountability to parents/school management in 84, **85**, *85*, 92; teachers' collectivism/individualism in 90, 92, **93**, 94, 138, 143; teachers' organizational support in 97' **98**, 99, *99*, **100**
Choo, S. S. 150
Cochran-Smith, M. 3
Coget, J.-F. 131
Cohen, J. 74
collectivism: accountability and 18–21; by country **90**, **91**, 91, *92*, **93**, **94**, 138, *139*, 140, *139*; at country level 21–22, *139*; cultural values and 17–18, **90**; by gender 94–95; individualism *vs.* 143, 150; in-group 30, 139, *139*, 140–141, **141**, *141*; mean distribution 90–92, **90**, **91**, *91*, *92*; predicting accountability by 101–122, **102**, **104**, **107**, **109**, **110**, **111**, **115**, **116**, **118**, **119**, 131–135; predicting principals' accountability by 114–122, **116**, **119**; predicting teachers' accountability by 108–114, **110**, **111**; principal gender differences for **96**; principals and 20, **94**, *139*; seniority and 96–97, **97**; study measure of 29–31; teacher gender differences for **95**; teachers and 20, **93**, 135, *139*
colonialism 136
control 12
Conway, S. L. 14
cultural values: accountability and 16–18; implications of 149–150; organizational behavior and 16–17; *see also* collectivism; individualism

Darling-Hammond, L. 3, 137, 149, 151
Davis, E. 28
Davis-Blake, A. 15, 129
Dizon-Ross, R. 147
Drach-Zahavi, A. 7, 16
Dubnick, M. J. 11, 12
Dubrin, A. J. 11, 14

Earley, P. C. 17, 18, 21, 152–153
Easley, J. II 2, 16, 137
educational boards 9–10, 12, 20, 130; *see also* school boards; school management
Egger, J. 13, 130, 151
Ehren, M. C. 142
Eisenberger, R. 23, 31, 143
Elmore, R. F. 148
Enders, C. K. 33
Eraut, M. 11
Erez, M. 17, 18, 21
Erichsen, K. 147, 148
Every Student Succeeds Act (ESSA) 2, 3
Exchange Theory 24, 144

Farooqi, M. T. K. 23
Feldman, S. B. 3, 10, 11, 125, 134
felt accountability 1, 9, 23, 144; *see also* subjective accountability
Ferris, G. R. 6–7, 14, 15, 16, 29, 126, 148
Firestone, W. A. 3, 9, 10, 11, 16, 29, 125, 134, 148, 151
Freeman, R. 12–13
Friedman, N. 13
Frink, D. D. 4, 6, 7, 14, 15, 16, 29, 126, 148
Fullan, M. 10, 150
Furman, G. C. 132

Gardner, W. C. 14–15
Garofalo, O. 4
Gelfand, M. J. 4, 16, 17–22, 29, 131, 133, 145, 149–150, 152
gender differences: accountability and 79–81, **80**, **81**; for collectivism **95**, **96**; for external accountability **80**, **82**; for individualism **95**, **96**; for internal accountability **81**, **82**;

Index

organizational support by **98**, 99, *99*, 100, **100**, 101, 146; predicting principals' accountability by **116**, **119**; predicting teachers' accountability by **110**, **111**

Gibton, D. 20, 136

Global Leadership and Organizational Behavior Effectiveness (GLOBE) project 30–31, 139, 140, **141**, *141*

goal orientation 8

Gouldner, A. 24, 144

Greenfield, P. M. 22

Grinshtain, Y. 14, 20, 151

Halkias, D. 14

Hall, A. T. 1, 6–7, 9, 16, 23, 25, 126, 144

Hallinger, P. 125

Hareli, S. 7, 153

Heintz, P. 8

Hernández, F. 2–3, 136, 137, 148

Herr, R. M. 153

hierarchical linear models (HLM) 32, 74, 115, 133, 141, 152

Hill, R. B. 11

Hochwarter, W. 9, 16

Hofstede, G. 16, 18, 21–22, 30

Hornby, G. 130

House, R. J. 16, 18, 21–22, 30, 131

Hox, J. J. 32, 34

Huang, F. 17

Hungary: collectivism in *139*, *141*; data collection on 30, 34, 27, **27**, 138; gender differences in accountability in **80**, **81**, 82, 94, **95**; principals' accountability in **76**, 77, 79, **79**, 80, 83, 95, **136**; principals' accountability to parents/school management in **86**, **87**, *87*, **88**, **89**, *89*; principals' collectivism/individualism in **91**, *92*, **94**; principals' organizational support in **98**, 99, **100**; seniority and accountability in **83**; seniority and individualism/collectivism in 97; teachers' accountability in 75, *76*, 78, **79**, 88, *88*, 135–136; teachers' accountability to parents/school management in **85**, *85*, **87**, *88*, **89**, *89*; teachers' collectivism/individualism in **90**, 92, **93**, 94; teachers' organizational support in **98**, *99*, **100**

IBM Corp. 30

Impression Management Theory 7, 14–15

individualism: accountability and 18–21; collectivism *vs.* 143, 149–150; by country 90–94, **90**, **91**, *91*, *92*, **93**, 138–140; at country level 21–22; cultural values and 17–18; by gender 94–95; mean distribution 90–92, **90**, **91**, *91*, *92*; predicting accountability by 101–122, **102**, **104**, **107**, **109**, **110**, **111**, **115**, **116**, **118**, **119**, 131–135; predicting principals' accountability by 114–122, **116**, **119**; predicting of teachers' accountability by 108–114, **110**, **111**; principal gender differences for **96**; principals and 20, **94**, *139*; seniority and 96, 97; study measure of 29–31; teacher gender differences for **95**; teachers and 20, **93**

in-group collectivism *see* collectivism

internal accountability *see* accountability

Israel: collectivism in *139*, *141*; data collection on 27, **27**, 138; gender differences in accountability in **80**, **81**, **82**, 94, 95; principals' accountability in **76**, 77, 79, **79**, **80**, 83, 95, **116**, **119**, 136; principals' accountability to parents/school management in **86**, **87**, *87*, **88**, **89**, *89*; principals' collectivism/individualism in **91**, *92*, **94**; principals' organizational support in **98**, *99*, **100**; seniority and accountability in **83**; seniority and individualism/collectivism in 97; teacher gender differences in **80**, **81**, **95**; teachers' accountability in 75, *76*, 78, **78**, **79**, 84, *88*, 135–136; teachers' accountability to parents/school management in 84, **85**, *85*, **87**, *88*, **89**, *89*; teachers' individualism/collectivism in **90**, 92, **93**; teachers' organizational support in **98**, *99*, **100**

Index   167

Jiang, H. 17–18
job satisfaction 15, 23–24

Keddie, A. 149
Khanolainen, D. 128
Kim, U. 131
Kitayama, S. 17
Klimoski, R. J. 4
Knapp, M. S. 3, 10, 11, 125, 134
Krejsler, J. 125
Kristof, A. L. 147

Lafaele, R. 130
Laird, C. 7
Lareau, A. 14, 130
Larson, R. B. 127–128
Lavrakas, P. J. 127–128
Leader-Member Exchange (LMX) Theory 131
legitimacy 7–8, 130, 144, 151
Lee, J. 3
Leng, C.-H. 128
Leonenko, M. 9
Lerner, J. S. 4, 6
Liu, Y. 24
Lortie, D. C. 126
Luria, G. 153

Maas, C. J. 32, 34
Markus, H. 17
Martinko, M. J. 14–15
McNall, L. A. 15
Meyers, M. C. 23
Miller, M. J. 11
morality 11, 132, 142, 149
Moran, R. M. R. 148
Morris, R. J. 18
Mpungose, J. E. 136
Müller, J. 2–3, 136, 137, 148
Muñoz, V. L. 14, 130

Nataly, P. D. 23
National Commission on Excellence in Education 2
Netherlands, the: collectivism in *139*, *141*; data collection on 27, **27**, 138; gender differences in accountability in 80, 94; principal accountability in 76, 76–79, *77*, *79*, **80**, 83, 86–88, 117, 120, 136, 141–142, **141**, *141*;

principal accountability to parents/school management in 84, **86**, *87*, *88*, 118–120, **118**, **119**; principal collectivism/individualism in 90, 91, *91*, **92**, 93, **93**, 94, *94*, **94**; principal organizational support in **98**, 99, *99*, **100**; seniority and accountability in 83, **83**; seniority and collectivism/individualism in 97; teacher accountability in 75, 75–76, *76*, 78, **78**, 79, 84, *88*, 135–136, 142; teacher accountability to parents/school management in 84, **85**, *85*, **87**, 88, *88*, 143; teacher collectivism/individualism in 90, *91*, 92, 93, **93**, 94, **95**, 97, 143; teacher organizational support in **98**, *99*, **100**
Ngwenya, T. H. 136
No Child Left Behind (NCLB) policy 2, 125–126

objective accountability 8, 15–16
OECD 127, 138, 142, 146
organizational behavior 4, 16–17, 24–25, 146, 150
organizational support: accountability and 22–25; background variables of 146; by country 97–99, **98**, *99*, **100**, 145–146; definition of 23; by gender **98**, 99–101; job attitudes/behaviors and 24; mean distribution of 97–99, **98**, *99*; predicting principals' accountability by **116**, **119**; predicting teachers' accountability by 106, **110**, **111**, 112; principals and **98**, 99, *99*, 144–145; by seniority 99–101, **100**; study methods of 31; teachers and **98**, 99, 144; work attitudes/behaviors and 24; *see also* school support
Oser, F. 11

Papagianni, A. 14
parent organizations 130
parents: accountability to school management *vs*. 129–130; informal power of 14–15; prediction of accountability to 118, **118**, **119**, 120, 123, 134–135; principals and 14; principals' accountability to 83–88,

84, 86, *87*, **87**, *88*; as stakeholders 13, 151; teachers' accountability to 83–88, **85**, *85*, **86**, **87**, 87, *88*, 108–113, **110**, **111**, 122; unique status of 130
Parimah, A. 17
Pascual, M. A. C. 127
Peeters, M. 35
perceived accountability 129, 132–133, 147
Perera, H. B. 4, 19, 22, 133, 150, 152
performance standards/evaluations 2–3, 7–8, 15, 29, 127; *see also* school performance; work performance
personal accountability *see* accountability
Petty, G. C. 11
Pfeffer, J. 15, 129
Poulson, L. 10–11, 125, 134, 148
principals: collectivism/individualism by country **94**; cultural values and **91**, 91–93, *92*, 95, **96**, **97**; cultural values mean distribution **91**; gender differences in accountability **82**; gender differences in cultural values 95–96, **96**; gender differences in organizational support **98**, 100–101; job satisfaction of 23–24; organizational commitment of 24; organizational support and 97–99, **98**, *99*, 100–101, **100**, 144–145; parental involvement and 14; parent organizations and 130; professional responsibility of 125; study questionnaire 42–48
principals' accountability: by country **76**, 76–79, **77**, **80**, *85*, 86–88, **86**, **87**, *87*, **88**, **89**, *89*, 136, *141*; and effects on/predicting of teachers' accountability 106–108, **107**, **111**, 113–114, 131; gender differences and 81, **82**; to parents 86–88, **86**, **87**, *87*, **88**, 118–120, 123, 130; regression models for **116**, **119**; to school management 86–88, **86**, **87**, *87*, **89**, *89*, 114, 120–121, 123
professional accountability *see* accountability
professionalism 11–12

questionnaires: for principals 42–48; study variables 50; for teachers 36–42

Rasmussen, P. 136, 146
Raudenbush, S. W. 32
Realo, A. 19
Reciprocity Theory 24, 144
responsibility, defined 7; *see also* accountability
Reynolds, J. 147, 148
Rhodes, L. 23
Riantoputra, C. 23, 144
Roch, S. G. 15
Rosenblatt, Z. 3, 4, 15, 16, 28–29

Saris, H. 13
Schlenker, B. R. 8
school boards 7, 24, 97, 130, 145; *see also* educational boards
school community 132–133, 150
school leadership 2–3, 137; *see also* educational boards; principals; school management
school management: accountability to parents *vs.* 129–130; prediction of accountability to 118, **118**, **119**, 120, 121, 123, 134–135; principals' accountability to 83–88, **84**, **86**, *87*, **87**, **88**, **89**, 114, 120–121, 123; teachers' accountability to 83–88, **85**, *85*, **86**, **87**, *88*, **89**, 108, **110**, **111**, 113–114, 122, 144
school performance 126, 145
school stakeholders 13, 15, 126, 129, 132, 137, 148, 151; *see also* parents; school management
school support 113, 135, 144, 146, 148; *see also* organizational support
Schwartz, S. H. 17
Scott, J. A. 14
Seashore-Louis, K. 3
Sefika, M. S. 11–12, 149
self-accountability 20
self-control 12
seniority: accountability and 81, 83, **83**; cultural values and 96, 97, **97**; organizational support by 99–101, **100**, 146; predicting principals' accountability by **116**, **119**;

predicting teachers' accountability by **110, 111**
Sezgin-Nartgün, S. 14
Shackleton, N. 142
Shaw, J. C. 7, 153
Shaw, R. D. 148
Shimoni, O. 3, 4, 15
Shipps, D. 3, 8–10, 11, 16, 29, 125, 134, 148, 151
Smetackova, I. 132, 153
Snyder, J. 149, 151
Social Contagion Theory 153
social desirability bias 127–128
Social Exchange Theory 24
social loafing 152–153
Somech, A. 131
Sora, B. 153
South Africa: collectivism in *139, 141*; data collection on 27–28, 74, 138; gender differences in accountability in 80, 94; principal accountability in **76**, 76–79, *77*, **79**, **80**, 117–118, 120, 136, 141–142, *141*; principal accountability to parents/school management in 86–88, **86**, *87*, *88*, 118–120, **118, 119**; principal collectivism/individualism in **90**, 91, *91*, **92**, 93, **93**, 94, *94*, **94**; principal organizational support in 97–99, **98**, 99, *99*, **100**; seniority and accountability in 81, 83, **83**; seniority and collectivism/individualism in **97**; teacher accountability in **75**, 75–76, *76*, 78, **78, 79**, 84, *88*, 135–136, 141; teacher accountability to parents/school management in 84, **84, 85**, *85*, **87**, 88, **88**, 143; teacher collectivism/individualism in 90, **90**, *91*, 92, 93, **93**, 94, **95**, **97**, 138; teacher organizational support in **98**, *99*, **100**, 101
Spain: collectivism in *139, 141*; data collection on 27, **27**, 138; gender differences in accountability in 80, 94; principal accountability in **76**, 76–79, *77*, **79**, **80**, 86, 117–118, 120, 136, 141–142, *141*; principal accountability to parents/school management in 86–88, **86**, *87*, *88*, 118–120, **118, 119**; principal collectivism/individualism in **90**, **91**, *91*, **92**, 93, **93**, 94, *94*, **94**; principal organizational support in 97–99, **98**, *99*, **100**, 101, 145–146; seniority and accountability in 83, **83**; seniority and collectivism/individualism in **97**; teacher accountability in **75**, 76, *76*, 78, **78, 79**, 84, 88, *88*, 135–136; teacher accountability to parents/school management in 84, **84, 85**, *85*, **87**, 88, **88**; teacher collectivism/individualism in **90**, *91*, 92, 93, **93**, 94, **95**, **97**, 138; teacher organizational support in **98**, 99, *99*, **100**
spillover effect 131
Stakeholder Theory 12–13
Starrat, R. J. 132, 150, 153
Staw, B. M. 15
Steele-Johnson, D. 8
stress 148
study methods: and accountability measures 28–29; and analytical approach 31–34; and background variables 31; and country-level values 30–31; and data collection 27–28; and individualism and collectivism measures 29; and individual-level values 29–30; and leveled structure teacher data 52; and missing data 35; and organizational support measure 31; and predicting accountability dispositions 32–34; and principal questionnaire 42–48; and teacher questionnaire 36–42
subjective accountability 4, 9, 16, 147–148, 152; *see also* felt accountability
Sugrue, C. 11–12, 149
Suh, E. M. 18
system accountability 9

teachers: collectivism/individualism by country **93**; cultural values and 90–94, **90**, *91*, **93**; cultural values mean distribution **90**; gender differences in accountability **80, 81**; gender differences in cultural values 94; gender differences in organizational support **98**, 99–101; parental involvement and 13–14; as semi-professional occupation 125

teachers' accountability: by country 75, 75–78, *76*, **78**, **79**, 84–88, **84**, **85**, *85*, **87**, *88*, *89*, 135–136, *141*; external **78**, 112–114; gender differences and 79–81, **80**, **81**; to parents 84–88, **85**, *85*, **87**, *87*, *88*, 112–113, 122; to school management 84–88, **85**, *85*, **89**, *89*, 113–114, 122; to students 3

Teaching and Learning International Survey (TALIS) 24, 127, 138, 146

team accountability 152–153

Teo, T. 17

Tetlock, P. E. 4, 6, 15

Thoms, P. 16

Tofighi, D. 33

transparency 7

Triandis, H. C. 17, 18, 29, 131, 143, 149–150

Tulowitzki, P. 2, 16, 137

Valli, L. 3

Van Buuren, S. 35

van Tartwijk, J. 142

Velayutham, S. 4, 19, 22, 133, 150, 152

Vincent, C. 13, 151

Wang, F. 24

Watson, P. J. 18

Weathers, J. M. 135

Weigold, M. F. 8

Welzel, C. 22

Wenderow, M. 131

Wikhamn, W. 23, 25, 144

Winston, B. E. 16

Wong, K. K. 3

Wood, J. A. 16

work attitudes/behaviors 15, 23–24, 143

work ethic 11

work experience 109, 112; *see also* seniority

work outcomes 130

work performance 7, 9, 23, 152–153

work team 153

Wubbels, T. 142

Yilmaz, K. 18

Zamir, S. 127

Zeinabadi, H. R. 131

Zimbabwe: collectivism in *139*, *141*; data collection on 27, **27**, 30, 31; gender differences in accountability in 80, 94; principal accountability in **76**, 76–79, *77*, **79**, **80**, 87–88, 136, **141**, *141*; principal accountability to parents/school management in 86–88, **86**, *87*, *88*, 118–120, **119**; principal collectivism/individualism in **90**, **91**, *91*, **92**, 93, **93**, 94, **94**, *94*; principal organizational support in **98**, 99, *99*, **100**; seniority and accountability in 83, **83**; seniority and collectivism/individualism in **97**; teacher accountability in **75**, 76, *76*, 78, **78**, **79**, 84, 88, *88*, 135–136; teacher accountability to parents/school management in 84, **84**, **85**, *85*, **87**, 88, **88**; teacher collectivism/individualism in 90, **90**, 91, *91*, 92, 93, **93**, 94, **95**, **97**, 138; teacher organizational support in 83, **98**, *99*, **100**

Zohar, D. 153

Zou, Y. 136, 146